Contents

Key to features

 ACTIVITY
A practical task to help you to understand Descartes' ideas.

▶ criticism ◀
Highlights and evaluates some of the difficulties Descartes faced.

 experimenting with ideas
Plays around with some of the concepts discussed; looks at them from different angles.

A direct quotation from one of Descartes' books.

 more difficult
A more in-depth discussion of Descartes' work.

Read
Meditations pages
Highlights the key pages of the *Meditations* that you should read before continuing with this book.

The series

This series is for students who are beginning to study philosophy. The books fill the middle ground between introductory texts, which do not always provide enough detail to help students with their essays and examinations, and more advanced academic texts which are often too complex for students new to philosophy to understand.

All of the study guides are written around the themes and texts for the AQA AS level philosophy specification. In addition to Descartes' *Meditations* there are five other guides:

- Plato's *Republic*
- Philosophy of Religion
- Sartre's *Existentialism and Humanism*
- Epistemology: the Theory of Knowledge
- Moral Philosophy

The authors have substantial experience of teaching philosophy at A level. They are also committed to making philosophy as accessible and engaging as possible. The study guides contain exercises to help students to grasp the philosophical theories and ideas that they'll face.

Feedback and comments on these study guides would be welcome.

Notes on the text

This book is best read alongside the *Meditations* and we give the relevant page and/or paragraph numbers that you should study for each chapter in the margin. All references to the *Meditations* are to the Penguin Classics edition, in *Discourse on Method and the Meditations*, 1968 (ISBN 0140442065), translated from the Latin by F. E. Sutcliffe.

Before publishing his work, Descartes arranged for his friend, Mersenne, to circulate it amongst various leading thinkers of the day, so that they could make critical comments on his arguments. These *Objections* along with Descartes' *Replies* accompanied the text when it first appeared and provide a useful resource, both for exploring difficulties with it and for better understanding Descartes' intentions. While the *Objections* and *Replies* are not included in the Penguin edition we use, they can be found in many collections of Descartes' work and we do make reference to them here.

Words in SMALL CAPITALS are defined in the Glossary on pages 163–8.

The Meditations
René Descartes

Daniel Cardinal
Jeremy Hayward
Gerald Jones

Academic consultant
Andrew Pyle

der Murray
THE HODDER HEADLINE GROUP

Authors

Daniel Cardinal is Head of Philosophy at Orpington College; **Jeremy Hayward** is a lecturer at the Institute of Education, University of London; **Gerald Jones** is Head of Humanities at the Mary Ward Centre, London.

The academic consultant **Andrew Pyle** is Senior Lecturer in Philosophy at the University of Bristol. He is the author of *Malebranche*, published 2003, in Routledge's 'Arguments of the Philosophers' series.

Acknowledgements

Extracts from *Discourse on Method and the Meditations* by René Descartes translated with an introduction by F. E. Sutcliffe (Penguin Classics, 1968). Copyright © F. E. Sutcliffe, 1968.

Cover photo © Bettmann/Corbis.

Although every effort has been made to ensure that website addresses are correct at time of going to press, Hodder Murray cannot be held responsible for the content of any website mentioned in this book.

Hodder Headline's policy is to use papers that are natural, renewable and recyclable products and made from wood grown in sustainable forests. The logging and manufacturing processes are expected to conform to the environmental regulations of the country of origin.

Orders: please contact Bookpoint Ltd, 130 Milton Park, Abingdon, Oxon OX14 4SB. Telephone: +44 (0)1235 827720. Fax: +44 (0)1235 400454. Lines are open from 9.00a.m. to 5.00p.m., Monday to Saturday, with a 24-hour message answering service. Visit our website at www.hoddereducation.co.uk

First published in 2006
by Hodder Murray, an imprint of Hodder Education,
a member of the Hodder Headline Group
338 Euston Road
London NW1 3BH

Impression number   10 9 8 7 6 5 4 3 2
Year   2010 2009 2008 2007 2006

Artwork by Oxford Illustrators Ltd
Cover design by John Townson/Creation
Typeset in 11/13 Galliard by Dorchester Typesetting Group Ltd,
Dorchester, Dorset
Printed and bound in Malta

A CIP catalogue record for this title is available from the British Library

ISBN-10: 0 340 88804 0
ISBN-13: 978 0 340 88804 9

Introduction

Descartes' *Meditations on First Philosophy* is one of the most significant texts in the history of western philosophy. Its project is ambitious, for in it Descartes attempts to establish the foundations for the whole of human KNOWLEDGE and describe, in outline, the framework within which the sciences would develop. Along the way he calls into question the very existence of the physical universe; attempts to prove the existence of GOD; discovers the essential nature of matter and provides an account of the relation of body and soul. In so doing Descartes set the agenda for debate in much of modern philosophy.

Given its significance within a discipline known for the profound and complex nature of its subject matter, one might expect the *Meditations* to be a particularly difficult read. And it is true that much of the book is steeped in the medieval jargon of Descartes' forebears and deals in the kind of knotty argumentation which professional philosophers make a living out of unpicking. However, on reading its opening passages, the lay reader is immediately struck by the freshness of Descartes' approach and by the immediacy and accessibility of the ideas.

The work describes the intellectual voyage of its author, from his initial state of ignorance, via an intense SCEPTICISM which shatters his BELIEF system to the core, and along a painstaking and arduous journey of discovery. Through the first-person narrative Descartes invites the reader to join him on this journey so that we quickly become fellow travellers: coming to understand for ourselves the urge to discovery that inspired him, described in the opening paragraphs; the dejection of his early scepticism where prospects for success seem bleak; the trials and tribulations encountered along the way; and the ultimate triumph as we arrive at our destination. The style and content of the *Meditations* conspire to give this work a timeless and universal quality, as the reader treads the same paths as did Descartes four hundred years ago.

Here our purpose is to help the reader join Descartes on his journey. But he would not want us to follow him blindly. For Descartes, truly following a train of thought involves carefully considering each step for ourselves before we take it.

So, for our pursuit to be worthwhile, it must be a critical and reflective one. This will mean that you may not always be persuaded by Descartes' arguments, and in the end you may find you are unconvinced that his ambitions have been realised. But, whether or not Descartes finally succeeds, the attempt is a heroic one, and hopefully you will find that the quest itself will have been worthwhile.

The bulk of the text here is concerned directly with the detail of the arguments of the *Meditations*. However, we will begin first with some background detail on Descartes the man and the world he inhabited. This introductory section is offered with some caution, for, as we have seen, Descartes intended his text to transcend the particular time and place in which he lived. The truths he hoped to establish were to be universal and timeless and so should stand or fall on their own merits, independently of their historical genesis. Whether such an ambition is ever truly achievable is itself a matter of some philosophical dispute. Many would claim that philosophers' ideas are in reality a product of their time, regardless of the claims they may make for them. If this is true then biographical detail and background may help us gain a better understanding of the text. However, Descartes would certainly have wanted you to skip this introduction, leap straight into the *Meditations* and examine the arguments on their own terms.

The choice, of course, is yours.

Background and context

Descartes' life

In 1596 René Descartes was born into a professional and relatively wealthy family living in La Haye, a small town in the north-west of France. At around the age of nine, the young Descartes was sent to study at a nearby Jesuit college in La Flèche. Because of ill health, Descartes was allowed the unusual privilege of lying in bed until 11a.m. each morning – a habit that stayed with him for the rest of his life. At this time the Jesuits were known as the schoolmasters of Europe and Descartes was lucky enough to study classics, Aristotelian physics and, later, mathematics, for which he showed great natural ability. It is believed that Descartes then went on to study law at the University of Poitiers.

His studies completed, Descartes travelled to Holland to enlist as a volunteer in the army of Prince Maurice of Nassau, effectively becoming a cadet in a military academy (military service was a tradition in his family). Although for the next few years Descartes served under different armies, it must be pointed out that this was always as a volunteer. He received no pay, and part of his motive was the opportunity a military career provided both to think and to travel. After all, actual fighting was not likely for someone of Descartes' background. During this period, Descartes made a close friend in Doctor Isaac Beeckman, who reawakened Descartes' early interest in maths and science.

In 1619 Descartes left the military academy in Holland and travelled round Europe to Germany where he joined the army of Maximilian of Bavaria. Throughout this time Descartes became increasingly preoccupied with mathematical issues and eventually became convinced that he had solved many longstanding problems. A period of particularly intense thinking culminated on 10 November 1619 when, shut away in a small stove-heated room in Germany, Descartes claimed to have experienced a series of visions, which he interpreted as bestowing on him a divine mission to seek the truth through the use of REASON.

For the next five years Descartes continued his military service in Bohemia and Hungary. In 1623 he left the army and travelled further around Europe, settling in Paris in 1626 where he mixed in fairly lofty intellectual circles. However, he found social life in Paris very distracting and in 1628 moved to Holland, where, other than for occasional visits to France, he remained for the next twenty-one years.

All this time Descartes was still motivated by his mission to seek the truth through reason. While in military service – and again in Paris – Descartes had been making important (but unpublished) breakthroughs in mathematics. Based on his vision in 1619, he was convinced that he was able to make these breakthroughs because of the particular mode in which he approached the problems. He felt it was the rational method he was applying that was the key and, further, that this method could be used, beyond mathematics, to seek out the truth in many other areas of human thought.

While in Paris he started formulating this new method in great detail, many elements of which he claimed came to him that night in 1619. However, the book he was writing – *Rules for the Direction of the Mind* – was never completed and was not published until after his death.

While trying to articulate his new method he was still busy applying it to try to solve problems not only in mathematics but also in science and philosophy. Settled in Holland, Descartes spent years working on an ambitious project – the *Traité du monde* (*Treatise on the World*) – a treatise that would lay out a unified theory of the physical universe. However, in 1633 the famous scientist Galileo was condemned by the inquisition in Rome for his recent publication on astronomy, which, like the earlier astronomer Copernicus, placed the sun at the centre of the planetary system with the earth, moon and planets in orbit around it. This contradicted the previously accepted theory of Ptolemy, that the planetary system was earth-centred with the planets moving round the earth in circular orbits. The Catholic Church regarded the earth-centred model as an important article of faith, as it reflected man's place at the centre of God's design for the universe. Galileo was condemned for teaching the Copernican theory and spent the rest of his days under house arrest. Descartes' book, nearly ready for print, also placed the sun at the centre of the universe. Because this claim formed such an integral part of his system this could not easily be edited out, and so Descartes decided not to publish.

During the next few years Descartes started several new projects but none of them came to any real fruition. He also fathered an illegitimate daughter, who sadly died at the age of five, a tragedy which he claimed was the greatest sorrow of his life.

Rather than publish an all-encompassing work, which would necessarily include his heretical theories of planetary motion, Descartes chose to publish three short essays, each showing the application of his new method to a particular field of inquiry: *Geometry, Optics* and *Meteorology.* He accompanied these with another essay – the *Discourse on Method* – which, as well as giving an autobiographical account of his intellectual development and a summary of his views on philosophy and physics, also gives an account of the special method he had devised in order to reach the truth on any topic. An understanding of the *Discourse on Method* is important in establishing a context for the *Meditations* and so is dealt with in more detail at the end of this brief biography.

Descartes had great hopes for the *Discourse* and the accompanying essays. Not only could it establish him as a leading thinker, he also hoped that it would help pave the way for future works on physics and philosophy to be published without condemnation. He enjoyed some success. The *Geometry,* although baffling many readers, established Descartes as a mathematical genius.

However, various aspects of the essays and the *Discourse* were met with strong objections, and responding to these occupied Descartes for some time. Further, the reaction from the Church was lukewarm and in some cases hostile. It was clear that Descartes needed to strengthen his ideas on metaphysics in order to meet the objections and criticisms of both the philosophers and theologians.

To this end, in 1641 Descartes published the *Meditations on First Philosophy* which provided a more detailed account of his metaphysics. Once again he had high hopes for its success but again he was frustrated by what he saw as his readers' failure to understand the text. Descartes found himself again embroiled in answering and fending off damaging criticisms from various theologians, notably from the Jesuit scholars who had provided his education.

In 1644 he published his *Principles of Philosophy.* This work contained another summary of his views on philosophy, but also outlined many of his ideas on physics and cosmology from the unpublished *Traité du Monde.*

In 1649, at the age of 56, Descartes was invited to work in the court of Queen Christina of Sweden, a great admirer of his work. Although he initially declined, the ongoing philosophical and theological disputes over his work must have made the invitation seem more attractive, and Descartes, a devout Catholic, duly travelled to the Protestant court in Sweden.

Life in Sweden was not entirely to Descartes' liking. His philosophical services were rarely called upon – and when they were Queen Christina insisted that her lesson began at 5a.m. A renowned late riser since childhood, Descartes struggled with this regime. During the Swedish winter he became ill and died in February 1650.

After a slow start, Descartes' fame had grown steadily throughout his lifetime, particular in his later years. After his death he became increasingly renowned – indeed many Catholics thought he might be a candidate for sainthood. A measure of his fame is that during the transportation of his body from Sweden back to France, several pieces of his corpse were removed by relic collectors!

Background to the *Meditations*

Several aspects of Descartes' life help shed light on themes within the *Meditations*: his religious belief, his love of the new sciences and his preoccupation with the methods of mathematics. These and other topics are explored in more detail below. However, one aspect which we have already taken note of, and which is of particular relevance to the *Meditations,* is his interest in the concept of *order*. Descartes paid great attention to the timing of his publications. He was not one to rush his public by foisting a work upon them for which they might not be ready. And the concern for order is one of the most striking features of the *Meditations*. It is crucial in the book that its arguments are presented in their proper sequence so as to take the reader first through a series of sceptical arguments to undo our previous opinions, and then to derive each new discovery from the last so that, step by step, a system of unassailable truths might be built. This concern is reflected in the central metaphor he uses for his project in the *Meditations,* namely that of destroying a building of his former opinions through his scepticism, and then of rebuilding a new one, representing his new system of knowledge. There is only one order in which to construct a building – from the foundations up – and this is true also for Descartes' new system of knowledge. For this reason, unlike some other works of philosophy, it is not possible to dip in and out of the *Meditations*. Instead, the order in which his arguments develop is of paramount importance and means that the *Meditations* form an organic whole.

This concept of ensuring ideas are presented in the correct order not only is a defining feature of Descartes' thinking but also ushered in a whole new era of philosophy, which today is still known as the 'modern' period. What principally distinguishes post-CARTESIAN or 'modern' philosophy from that which went before is the increased importance of *method*. Questions about the correct way to gain knowledge begin to take centre stage. Before Descartes, philosophers' beliefs about the nature of the universe determined their ideas about what knowledge was and where it came from, rather than the other way round. In philosophical parlance, such philosophers had an ONTOLOGY (a view about the kinds of things that exist) and this dictated their EPISTEMOLOGY (their beliefs about how we can gain knowledge).

A classic example of such a philosopher is Plato, who, in the *Republic*, puts forward what is often termed a 'two-world view': a belief that, as well as the physical world which we observe with the senses, there exists a world of ideal 'forms' perceived by the mind. Plato then proceeds to define knowledge in terms of these forms, since genuine knowledge is supposed to involve apprehension of them. By contrast, the apprehension of the physical world by the senses amounts only to *opinion*. In this way Plato's *ontological* commitment to two worlds dictates the nature of his *epistemology*, that is to say, the way he contrasts knowledge and mere opinion.

Modern philosophy is in large part defined by a reversal of this procedure. Epistemology became 'first' philosophy and was placed before ontology. This meant that we had first to determine how we can acquire knowledge before we can make any pronouncement about what kinds of things exist in the universe. But Descartes was not alone in his focus on method. As he was writing, a new approach to scientific discovery was emerging in Europe. Increasingly, scientists of the period were employing the method of experimentation and exploiting the development of new technologies to aid their observations of the world. Galileo, for example, was the first to turn the newly invented telescope toward the planets and to discover by this method the existence of moons orbiting Jupiter: a new way of knowing the world determining a new understanding of what there is. Contrast this with the reaction of his inquisitors who refused to accept the evidence of the telescope essentially on the grounds that it did not fit in with the picture of the universe that tradition had handed down. For them, the way the universe operated and what existed was a given: established in large part by the revealed truths of the Bible.

Like Galileo, Descartes was keen to question the received wisdom of his contemporaries and in the *Meditations* Descartes tries to make a clean break from the past. In the opening lines he explicitly states that he will begin by ridding himself of his old beliefs about the nature of reality (in other words reject his current ontology); start again from scratch and then build up new beliefs using reliable methods (in other words deploying a new epistemology). In this way the *Meditations* represent a clean start for the whole of western philosophy, breaking from the beliefs of the past and starting again with a clean sheet.

Discourse on Method

Although the *Meditations* stand alone as a work of philosophy, the book represents an application of the method that Descartes had developed much earlier in his life. As we have seen, he outlines the nature of this method in a previous work: *Discourse on the Method of Rightly Conducting Reason and Reaching the Truth in the Sciences* published in 1637. The *Discourse*, along with its companion essays – *Geometry*, *Optics* and *Meteorology* – was supposed to show to the world, by example, his vision of a unified field of human knowledge based on foundations of certainty. As such, it represents the start of Descartes' efforts to fulfil his mission to disclose the truth through reason as revealed in his dreams of 1619.

The *Discourse*, as its full title suggests, sets out the general method that Descartes employs to reach truth. The remaining three essays show how the method can be applied to reach new truths in three different areas of human enquiry and the *Meditations* represent the application of the method in philosophy. The *Meditations* are particularly important in his grand scheme as their discoveries form the foundations to the whole of human knowledge and describe the framework within which all sciences will develop. In metaphorical terms, philosophy forms the trunk from which the other branches – geometry, optics, meteorology, etc. – will grow.

The *Discourse* is partly autobiographical, giving an account of Descartes' intellectual development, as well as summarising some of his previously unpublished scientific opinions. Part four of his *Discourse* contains a brief summary of his views on philosophy, and reads a little like a much shorter version of the *Meditations*. It is in this section, and not in the *Meditations* (as is often thought), that Descartes uses the famous phrase: *je pense, donc je suis*,[1] meaning 'I think, therefore I am'.

The discourse was written in French rather than Latin, expressly to appeal to an audience wider than just the academic community. Descartes was hoping that he would get a groundswell of support for his new ideas and method.

His 'revolutionary' method of achieving the truth is actually quite simple, involving just four rules.

1. *The first was never to accept anything as true if I had not evident knowledge of its being so; that is, carefully to avoid precipitancy and prejudice, and to embrace in my judgment only what presented itself to my mind so clearly and distinctly that I had no occasion to doubt it.*
2. *The second, to divide each problem I examined into as many parts as was feasible, and as was requisite for its better solution.*
3. *The third, to direct my thoughts in an orderly way; beginning with the simplest objects, those most apt to be known, and ascending little by little, in steps as it were, to the knowledge of the most complex; and establishing an order in thought even when the objects had no natural priority one to another.*
4. *And the last, to make throughout such complete enumerations and such general surveys that I might be sure of leaving nothing out.*[2]

By following these precepts, and ensuring that 'we avoid accepting as true what is not so, and always preserve the right order of deduction of one thing from another, there can be nothing too remote to be reached in the end, or too well hidden to be discovered'.[3]

In sum what Descartes is saying here is that we can discover any truth so long as we:

1 accept only beliefs that can be recognised clearly and distinctly to be true;
2 break down every problem into the smallest parts;
3 build up the arguments systematically in the right order;
4 carefully check through to ensure no steps are left out.

Descartes thought these principles had proved themselves in geometry and mathematics, and could also be used in the physical sciences and philosophy. It will be worth dwelling on just how useful these rules really are, since, as we've seen, the *Meditations* can be regarded as Descartes' attempt to apply them in the field of philosophy.

▶ criticism ◀ Turning to the first rule, we may ask just how CLEAR AND DISTINCT must a belief seem before we can be certain of its truth? In other words, how can we be sure that what seems to be clearly knowable in this way really is? We will be discussing Descartes' notion of 'clear and distinct' ideas and beliefs in more detail later (page 82ff. of this book), and one criticism that we will develop is that it is very hard to articulate with any precision which beliefs are to count as clearly and distinctly knowable.

▶ criticism ◀ A second problem is that Descartes' rules are just too vague to be of any but the most general use. It seems sensible to break down a problem into its smallest parts, but how are we to be sure that we have done so? Isn't it always going to be possible to break a problem down further? And while it seems sensible to proceed in the proper order, how are we to determine that we are doing so? And we will surely concur with Descartes that it is a good idea to check our workings, but just how careful do we need to be to ensure that no mistakes have been made and that we have left nothing out? Another great philosopher, Leibniz, whose work followed soon after Descartes', criticised these rules for being so general and vague that they amounted to advising us to 'take what you need, and do what you should and you will get what you want'.[4]

▶ criticism ◀ A further question arises as to whether these laws can generate new substantial truths. Descartes was inspired to devise these rules through his knowledge of mathematics, and mathematics builds a system of truths by starting with simple propositions and building up to more complex ones. However, many philosophers would argue that mathematics alone can tell us nothing about what exists in the world or how it behaves. Such philosophers will argue that all mathematical truths are ultimately ANALYTIC in character, that is to say, they are reducible to identity statements, statements of the form $a = a$, and so are simply true by definition. To take a simple example, the PROPOSITION $2 + 3 = 5$ can be reduced to the claim that $5 = 5$, which is obviously true by definition. But if this is true of all mathematical truths, then they can only tell us about the meanings of the symbols used to express them and nothing substantive about the world. Indeed $2 + 3$ would be 5 even if the universe did not exist. So by applying this mathematical method to philosophy, it may be argued, Descartes is bound to fail to discover interesting truths about physical reality. His method can tell him only about his own ideas and the definitions of the terms he uses.[5]

However, Descartes definitely believed that his new method was capable of generating new and interesting truths about the nature of the physical world. Indeed he thought that this method could be used to build up an entire unified field of scientific knowledge. You can judge for yourself just how successful this method is by seeing how many new truths you judge it succeeds in generating in the *Meditations*.

Although Descartes' method is open to criticism, what is perhaps more significant is the fact that he had a systematic method in the first place. As outlined above this is a pivotal moment in the history of western philosophy – the moment that epistemology was placed ahead of ontology in philosophical procedures.

The world that Descartes lived in

Although many of the thoughts contained in the *Meditations* remain novel and fresh to this day we must remember that Descartes was writing over 350 years ago. And while we might expect an exploration of philosophical issues drawn from the very nature and condition of human existence to ring true throughout the ages, it is inevitable that many of the ideas and many of the strategies deployed in the *Meditations* reflect the conceptual terrain of the age in which they were written. Consequently, some understanding of the world in which Descartes lived, and the intellectual currents of his day will allow for a deeper appreciation of the text. To that end, in this section we will give an overview of the scientific and philosophical views which characterised the intellectual life of Descartes' times.

The scientific world

Before the sixteenth century, science as we would now recognise it had not advanced greatly since the ancient world. But by Descartes' day, a revolution was underway which was gradually replacing the old concepts and methods. This same revolution, as we have already seen, was also questioning some age-old assumptions about the structure of the universe and, as a result, science was heading for collision with the Church. Descartes felt this conflict keenly, and the tensions between the new science and the Church were to shape much of his public life. Descartes insisted he was on the side of the Church, and yet his work clearly also sides with the new science. Having a foot firmly in both camps, Descartes eventually became a pivotal figure (after his death) in helping establish a world view that would allow Church and science to live alongside one another.

So what was this new scientific revolution, and what was it replacing? To answer this, let's begin with a brief account of the old scientific world view. Before the ENLIGHTENMENT, science was largely based on medieval interpretations of the work of the ancient Greek philosopher Aristotle. This 'scholastic science', as it was termed, can be characterised, in part, by the two features described overleaf.

1 The scholastics tended to attempt to explain the behaviour of physical objects and substances by invoking a supposed property or quality that they possessed. For example, to caricature somewhat, it was 'explained' that objects fell towards earth because they had the property of 'heaviness'. Material objects were thought to move towards the centre of the earth, because this tendency, this heaviness, was a part of their essential nature. In a similar way, liquids were said to tend to cover a surface because they had the property of 'wetness'. And if looking for an account for why opium sends you to sleep, the answer would be because it is soporific, meaning simply that it has the tendency to induce sleep. Now, while at first glance, such explanations may seem convincing, a little reflection reveals that they are unhelpfully circular. Simply turning the behaviour in question (for example the tendency to fall downwards) into a property that the object has (its heaviness) completely fails to explain why the phenomenon occurs. If I say opium makes you sleepy because it is soporific, I am not telling you anything you don't already know. The explanation merely recasts in different terms the fact that the object displays the behaviour in question.

2 Alongside this, scholastic thinkers had what is known as a TELEOLOGICAL view of the universe. *Telos* is the ancient Greek word for 'end' or 'goal', and a teleological explanation of something tries to account for it in terms of its purpose or goal. Take, for example, a simple and common occurrence such as the sprouting of an acorn. What might a teleological explanation of this event look like?

■ **Figure 2.1**
Why did the acorn sprout?

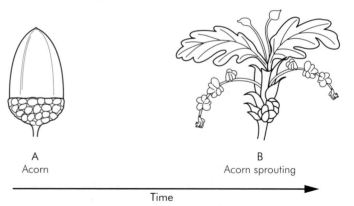

A
Acorn

B
Acorn sprouting

Time

A teleological explanation might run along the lines of: 'the shoot came out of the acorn because it was growing into a tree'. In other words, the future state towards which the acorn is developing – the full-grown oak tree – is being used to explain the present phenomenon.

■ **Figure 2.2
A teleological
explanation says B
happens because
of C**

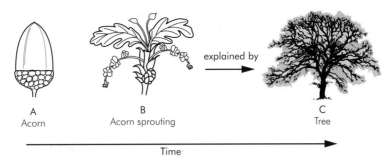

A
Acorn

B
Acorn sprouting

explained by →

C
Tree

Time →

This type of explanation of natural phenomena is pretty common to this day, especially when it comes to the behaviour of living things. We explain the appearance of blossom on trees in terms of the goal of attracting insects for fertilisation, and the growth of fruit as a means to achieve the goal of propagating seeds, and so on. It is as though processes such as these are driven by the final end to which they aspire. Now, such explanations are of particular importance within the Aristotelian view of the universe. On Aristotle's view all natural processes have a final resting point to which they are directed. So, he would explain the behaviour of the water in a river as it flows downstream in terms of its final resting place: the sea. The reason it flows down is in order to reach the sea. To see all processes teleologically is to see the universe as a bit like a snow shaker in which all the flakes are moving around, but ultimately heading for a final resting place. This teleological approach to natural science, when combined with the idea outlined above that all things have essential qualities which determine their behaviour, leads to a complete picture of the natural world in which everything has a certain nature revealed by its behaviour, and where such behaviour is explained in terms of the purpose of that thing.

The scientific revolution

During Descartes' life the influence of both these key ideas was in decline. Descartes, along with the other new scientists, thought that the scholastic way of explaining phenomena by reference to a myriad of qualities was largely useless. Chief among these new scientists was Galileo, who famously pronounced that the 'great book of the universe cannot be understood unless one can read the language in which it is written – the language of mathematics'.[6] For him, the true nature of the natural world was to be understood by using the clarity and precision of mathematics, rather than by appeal to obscure Aristotelian notions of essential qualities. Descartes similarly believed that, to explain how natural processes work and to describe the essential nature of material things,

13

arithmetic and geometry would be the unique tools. This meant that only those properties of reality which could be quantified and measured were to be included in a genuinely scientific account of the universe. Natural science would deal only in the measurable quantities of size, shape, number, speed and duration. Indeed, as Descartes argues in the *Meditations*, matter was in essence nothing more than what could be described geometrically. The appearance of any other qualities is a matter of obscurity and confusion.

This approach to science is still with us today. A good example of this is how a modern scientist would treat a phenomenon such as smell. Smells, scientists will claim, are caused by the different shapes of various molecules. As we breathe in, millions of molecules enter our nose. Our nose contains millions of receptors of different shapes and sizes. A molecule of the right shape may temporarily lodge itself into an appropriately shaped receptor, and, if enough of the same-shaped ones do this, then we experience a particular smell. So whereas a scholastic scientist would put the smell of bad eggs down to an invented quality, say 'egginess', a modern scientist would explain the smell by reference to the shape of the molecules in question, much in the manner suggested by Descartes and others.

In this new system, innumerable alleged qualities were abolished forever and replaced by a few measurable 'quantitative' properties. A second key feature of the new revolution was the rejection of teleological explanations in natural science and the insistence on what is termed 'mechanical' or 'efficient' causation. What this means is that instead of explanations being framed by reference to some future goal, the occurrence of any event was to be accounted for purely in terms of what immediately preceded it.

▓ **Figure 2.3** *B is explained by reference to A*

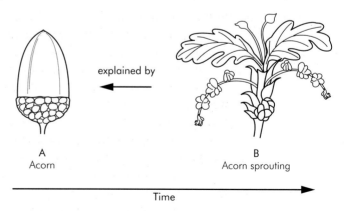

explained by

A
Acorn

B
Acorn sprouting

Time

Here the explanation for the acorn's sprouting is found in the state of things before the appearance of the shoot. Something in the acorn itself has caused the sprout to emerge and this cause is the unique explanation for the occurrence. In modern terms an explanation of this sort might run as follows: 'As the acorn takes in water from its surroundings, starches are caused to turn to sugars, in turn causing the sprout to expand to the point where the pressure inside is sufficient to cause the surface to break and out pops the shoot.' The present event is thus explained by reference to events in the immediate past rather than by events/states in some distant future.

Implicit in this way of thinking is the view that the state of the universe at any one moment is the direct result of the state of the universe the moment before in conjunction with the laws of the universe. This 'mechanical' or 'efficient' approach to explaining causation in the physical world gave credence to a new view of the universe, that of the universe as a complex machine, like a giant piece of clockwork. However, this new idea of the clockwork universe was not initially in tune with the thinking and preaching of the Church.

Science and the Church

Although a Catholic, Descartes was aware that many of his views, particularly those in physics but also those on philosophy, were not in keeping with the official doctrines of the Catholic Church. The Church's view of the universe was, to a large extent, based on the medieval reinterpretation of Aristotle's metaphysics. However, Descartes believed in the new science which, as we have seen, represents a rejection of the Aristotelian system. In resisting the new science, the Church's key objections were as follows:

■ The heliocentric (sun-centred) universe

Following on from the work of the Polish astronomer Copernicus, many of the new scientists viewed the sun, not the earth, as the centre of the planetary system. This shift had a huge impact on the way we view ourselves and our relationship with the universe. Before Copernicus, the earth was seen as the centre of the entire cosmos with everything from the sun and the moon to the five planets and the fixed stars revolving around it, which is to say, around *us*. After Copernicus, however, we are left with only the moon revolving around the earth. All the planets, including the earth, orbit the sun, and the fact that the sun appears to orbit the earth is caused by the spinning of the earth on its axis.

This radical shift in world view relegates humanity from the centre point of the whole of creation to its relative sidelines. And it was this which appeared incompatible with orthodox religious opinion. For if God created the universe and made man in his image, then surely we should occupy the centre stage. If the earth is the third of six known planets, then perhaps mankind was not the pinnacle of God's creation. Might there not even be life on the other planets? For various reasons this shift in focus was not acceptable to the Church at the time, despite the evidence revealed through Galileo's telescope.

The clockwork universe

The new heliocentric model of the universe made it much simpler to predict the movements of the planets with artificial devices. Mechanical and clockwork orreries (models of the solar system) became increasingly popular and these machines gave further credence to this emerging idea of a clockwork universe; an idea that represented another challenge to religious orthodoxy since it suggests that the universe can operate without the need for God's sustaining influence.

Science as intrusive

To some religious authorities, the very idea of the new science was a challenge. The prevailing view of human knowledge in Christian Europe, a view which had its roots in the philosophy of Plato, regarded genuine knowledge as concerned not with the physical world as perceived by the senses, but with some ideal or heavenly world comprehended by the mind. Knowledge is revealed to us by God, through scriptures and church teachings and it is not up to mankind to investigate nature in order to attempt to discover its secrets. If knowledge of the transient world in which we live is not actually possible then any efforts to explain its workings would be either futile or, worse, an offence against God.

Descartes was very nervous about offending the Church. He believed in the heliocentric model of the universe but deliberately held back from publishing his beliefs on this matter when Galileo was placed under house arrest. This nervousness is apparent in the dedication prefacing the *Meditations*, which Descartes offered to 'the learned and distinguished men, the dean and doctors of the sacred faculty of theology at Paris'. He is at pains to point out that the book itself is written to demonstrate to unbelievers the existence of God and the nature of the soul and thus urges the theologians to grant the *Meditations* their 'protection'.

Whether this is indeed the real purpose of the *Meditations* is a matter of some speculation. We should also remember that Descartes had the lofty ambition of establishing a new system of knowledge based on reason, and that the *Meditations* plays a key role in laying down the foundations of this new system. Perhaps this is its real purpose. Indeed, the exact nature and extent of Descartes' religious beliefs have been called in to question by some who perceive his religion as a useful device to avoid the sort of persecution that beset Galileo.

This book will not speculate on such matters. What is clear from reading the preface is that Descartes was very keen to avoid undue religious confrontation with the publication of the *Meditations* and that he possessed an acute awareness of the controversy caused by the new science and new ways of thinking.

The philosophical context

Throughout the dark ages the level of literacy in Europe was very low. Most of the people who could read and write were involved directly in the Church, often working in monasteries. Consequently, the Church was in effective control of intellectual development throughout Europe. In the thirteenth century Thomas Aquinas had attempted to marry the re-discovered writings of Aristotle with the preachings of the Church, and the resultant philosophy of Thomism still underpins Catholic teaching today. However, despite the great influence of Aristotle, philosophy remained focused on religious matters. That has led to the (probably fictional) accusation that philosophers of this period spent their time discussing such pressing issues as how many angels can be fitted on the head of a pin.

While philosophy did not advance greatly in the fourteenth and fifteenth centuries, society itself underwent huge upheavals. The Renaissance – a term for the burgeoning of arts and commerce from 1350 onwards – was spreading throughout Europe. In the larger coastal cities, a new middle class was rapidly developing. Neither landowners nor serfs, these doctors, merchants and craftsmen had a thirst for literature and knowledge, which in turn fuelled the demand for the printing press and educational establishments. A new wave of intellectuals working outside of religious institutions emerged, and Descartes was a classic example of this new breed.

Largely because of these changes in society, the seventeenth century saw a huge number of challenges to the status quo. Protestantism was spreading throughout northern Europe and the role of the Church was increasingly being questioned. The 'divine right of kings' – the view that monarchs held their positions because they were chosen by God – was also being challenged. Aristotelian science was being replaced, and the geocentric (earth-centred) view of the universe turned on its head. As the old ways of thinking were being undone, scepticism started to gain greater currency. If so many traditional beliefs have turned out to be false, then what is to say that most – or even all – of our current beliefs are not in fact false? Some even doubted that humans were capable of true knowledge about anything at all.

All of this philosophical background is reflected in the *Meditations*. We see the dominance of religious themes, the development of new ways of thinking and the exploration of scepticism. However, amidst all this philosophical scepticism, one area of enquiry continued to stand out as a beacon of truth in a world of uncertainty. The world of mathematics, as in the ancient world, was still regarded as representing the high point of human intellectual achievement: the one area of enquiry in which mankind had gained certainty and clarity.

Descartes and mathematics

As is evident from his biography, one of the biggest influences on the philosophy of Descartes was his love of mathematics. His love was not just that of an admirer: during his lifetime Descartes established himself as one of the world's leading mathematicians and has left a lasting influence in the field.

Descartes was the pioneer of coordinate geometry. Before him, geometry and algebra were separate disciplines. Descartes unified these using a method of analysing shapes, employing an *x* axis and a *y* axis which allowed geometry to be expressed and analysed algebraically. See Figure 2.4.

■ **Figure 2.4**
Any plane figure can be plotted using co-ordinates on two axes

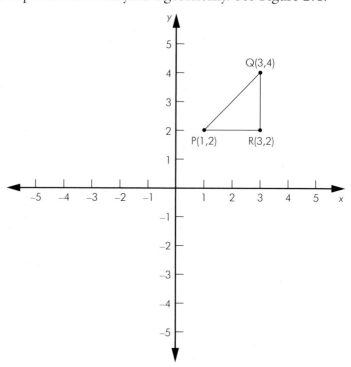

To this day, the *x* and *y* axes as shown in the diagram are referred to as Cartesian coordinates (Cartesian meaning 'of Descartes'). Descartes also devised the system of using *x*, *y* and *z* for unknown variables and *a*, *b* and *c* for known variables, as well as developing the standard of notations for cubes (^{3}) and roots ($\sqrt{}$).

Like many other philosophers, Descartes was impressed with the certainty that mathematics seemed to provide: 'I was especially delighted in mathematics because of the certainty and self-evidence of its readings.'[7] Descartes, guided by his visions of 1619, wanted this level of certainty to reach other areas of human knowledge and so used the methods of mathematics as a template for all knowledge. Two important elements from his work in mathematics stand out as key influences on the *Meditations*.

First is Descartes' success in unifying the fields of geometry and arithmetic. Although we can only speculate, the combining of two separate systems of knowledge into a unified theory is likely to have inspired his dream to develop a single unified system of all human knowledge, encompassing maths, science, philosophy and even ethics. His vision was for a single field of knowledge, with each area spreading out like branches on a tree. The *Meditations* represents Descartes' attempt to establish the trunk of that tree.

ACTIVITY   Let us take Descartes' metaphor of knowledge as a tree, supported by a trunk branching out into different disciplines. The most fundamental disciplines are at the base of the tree and the rest grow out of them. Those areas of knowledge at the outer branches rely on the trunk.

Where would *you* place the following disciplines? Which do you think are the most fundamental and which the least? Do they really all form part of one 'tree'? That is, is human knowledge part of a single unified field?

Biology
Chemistry
Ethics
French
Geography
History
Literary studies
Mathematics
Philosophy
Physics
Politics
Psychology
Religion
Sociology

An interesting parallel to this exists in the world of physics today where the systems of quantum mechanics (governing very small phenomena) and relativity (governing very large phenomena) are still separate and the Holy Grail of contemporary physics is to unify these in a single theory.

The second key influence of the world of mathematics in the *Meditations* is Descartes' employment of his method. We have already touched upon the basic rules he recommends, but to understand this method more fully we need briefly to explore the work of the seminal Greek mathematician Euclid.

In his book the *Elements*, Euclid sets out what is known as an axiomatic system, that is to say, a system in which all the propositions are derived from a small set of initial axioms and definitions. These initial axioms and definitions are thought to be self-evident. For example, among Euclid's axioms and definitions are the following:

All right angles equal one another.

A circle is a plane figure contained by one line such that all the straight lines falling upon it from one point among those lying within the figure equal one another.

From these he proceeds to prove a host of propositions concerning geometry, for instance:

If a straight line falling on two straight lines makes the alternate angles equal to one another, then the straight lines are parallel to one another.

Through the careful use of reason Euclid is able to establish a large and systematic body of truths all derived from his initial axioms and definitions.

Euclid's system was undoubtedly the inspiration behind Descartes' own method for achieving the truth. As set out in his *Discourse* (see above, p. 8), Descartes first wanted to discover clear and distinct ideas that cannot be doubted (axioms) and then, building from this point, to establish a complete system of truths. Descartes saw this as much more than a mathematical procedure, but as something that could be applied to the whole of science and philosophy.

These long chains of perfectly simple and easy reasonings by means of which geometers are accustomed to carry out their most difficult demonstrations had led me to fancy that everything that can fall under human knowledge forms a similar sequence.[8]

Descartes' philosophical approach

Descartes' philosophy has usually been classed as *rationalist* in character. Although there is no precise definition of RATIONALISM we can point to certain features that rationalist philosophies have in common. (For a fuller discussion of rationalism see *Epistemology: The Theory of Knowledge* in this series.) Most importantly rationalists argue that it is primarily by means of *reason*, rather than from authority or from sense experience, that knowledge of what exists or what is real is to be obtained. Rationalism is traditionally opposed to EMPIRICISM: the view that it is primarily through experience that knowledge is acquired. Rationalists also tend to argue that certain concepts are present in the mind prior to experience. For example, a rationalist might argue that we don't find out that the world contains substances or that events are caused by other events; rather the concepts of substance and cause are with us from the beginning. Lastly, rationalists tend to suppose that such knowledge can be fitted into a comprehensive and self-supporting system which will account (at least in essentials) for the nature of everything. In this it takes mathematics as its model of how knowledge ought to be structured.

The key difference between rationalists and empiricists lies in what they regard as the basic building blocks of knowledge. For the rationalist the building blocks are beliefs which are self-evident, beliefs that can be recognised as true just by thinking about them. For the empiricist they are beliefs derived from our sense experiences. This difference manifests itself when it comes to justifying any given piece of knowledge. Imagine both a rationalist and an empiricist believed in a particular scientific law, say the conservation of momentum, that is the idea that an object will keep moving in the same direction and with the same velocity unless acted on by another force. If we asked an empiricist how they know the law is true their answer would ultimately come down to observations and measurements of objects in motion, in other words, to sense experience.

But a rationalist would approach the question differently. They might justify the law by showing how it is derived from some more fundamental principle – perhaps the conservation of energy. Pressed further they might attempt to show how this principle is in turn derived from mathematical and geometrical principles. And when asked how they know these principles are true they might show how they are derived from other even more basic beliefs: beliefs that are beyond all doubt, and recognisable as true just by thinking about them. Whether this process is actually possible in reality is a moot point and most rationalists would recognise that some role for sense experience is necessary. After all, it is difficult to see how, if we have no information gained through the senses at all, we could possibly obtain the materials needed to acquire knowledge of the world. So most rationalist philosophers, and Descartes is no exception, recognise some role for sensation while nonetheless stressing that the most important knowledge of which we are capable is justified independently of any particular sense experience.

Traditionally, both rationalism and empiricism have been 'foundationalist' philosophies since they claim the basis for our knowledge has foundations that cannot be doubted. They simply disagree as to what these foundations are:

■ **Figure 2.5**
The empiricist believes that all of our knowledge of the world is constructed out of sense experience.

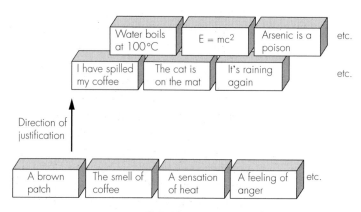

EMPIRICISM

THE FOUNDATIONS
Things we are immediately aware of such as colours, sounds and smells, as well as emotions and feelings; sometimes referred to as 'sense data' or the 'given'

■ **Figure 2.6**
The rationalist believes that our knowledge of the world is built using reason from basic indubitable beliefs.

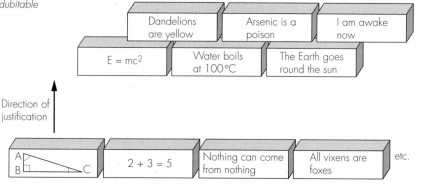

RATIONALISM

THE FOUNDATIONS: 'CLEAR AND DISTINCT' IDEAS
i.e. knowledge of maths and geometry; truths of reason and analytic truths

How might a) a strict rationalist and b) a strict empiricist go about explaining the foundations for the following claims:

1 That the earth goes around the sun
2 That two plus two equals four
3 That small objects (such as water bombs) fall towards very large objects (such as the earth) when dropped
4 That the internal angles of a triangle add up to 180 degrees
5 That there is a god.

The style of Descartes' *Meditations*

Descartes' *Meditations* are an attempt to bring his philosophy to a broad audience. They are immediately striking in that they use the first-person voice. But while this approach is in some ways very modern, it is not one without precedent. Writing meditations was already an established genre in the religious world. The technique was supposed to allow the reader to join the writer on a series of daily readings, contemplating different aspects of faith and spirituality. However, no one had ever used this method to write about philosophy. The device is, of course, deliberate: Descartes not only wants the reader to follow the text, he also wants the reader to think through the thoughts for themselves – to accompany him on a philosophical journey. Moreover, he wants the reader to take their time with the book, to read one meditation each day. By using the format of six meditations Descartes is asking for an in-depth and contemplative reading and expects the reader to reflect carefully on each move of the argument before being persuaded and moving on.

The first-person voice lends the *Meditations* an air of intimacy, as Descartes invites us into his inner thoughts. The thoughts he starts to explore involve reflection on the very basic beliefs about reality that we all share. The opening paragraphs offer a small amount of context for these thoughts. We learn that Descartes is no longer a young man, that he is alone, and that he has put aside some time to devote to this philosophical project. He is sitting by a fire, in a dressing gown, paper in hand. The homely detail, the lack of wider context and the familiarity of theme help to give the *Meditations* the sense that they could have been written any time, anywhere. This universality enhances the feeling that we are not simply reading the thoughts of Descartes, but that we are sharing them: embarking on our own quest for certainty.

It is also essential to remember that the overall structure of the *Meditations* is as important as the individual arguments. Descartes is trying to establish the foundations for a unified field of indubitable knowledge. So while each paragraph of the *Meditations* can be separately read and analysed, they are designed to form an organic whole. Descartes is trying to start from scratch and build a system of knowledge. If any one argument should fail, or should one set of conclusions not follow from the last, then there is the likelihood that he will have failed in his mission.

Having now set the scene, we are ready to embark upon the journey in thought described in Descartes' six *Meditations*. The overview on pages 25–27 provides a handy reminder. The central column gives a brief outline of Descartes' argument in the *Meditations*. The columns on either side highlight some of the issues surrounding the various stages and point to the pages where the relevant analysis can be found. (Please note that, in order to keep the overview brief, the portrayal of the central argument and the analysis of the various stages have been heavily edited and do not represent a full account.)

Overview of the *Meditations*

Comment	Central argument	Comment
Descartes begins his journey by doubting the evidence of his senses. However, is it really possible that he is always deceived by his senses? To be aware that you are sometimes deceived implies that on other occasions you are not deceived – how else would you have known you were deceived in the first place? Also, is it really possible he is dreaming all the time? A discussion of the different stages of doubt starts on page 29.	Some of my common-sense beliefs have been false.	In trying to start anew with his beliefs, Descartes proposes to subject his old beliefs to doubt. But what sort of doubt is he employing here and is it sincere? Is it really possible to doubt all your beliefs? Is it too much to ask for doubt-free beliefs? For an analysis of Descartes' method of doubt see page 29.
	I will start anew by subjecting all my beliefs to doubt and seeing if any remain doubt-free.	
	I doubt the evidence of my senses because: a) sometimes I am deceived by them b) I may be dreaming.	Descartes puts forward his Evil Demon Hypothesis. Is it really possible though for Descartes to doubt everything – even his basic reasoning? If it is impossible to tell if there is a demon or not, does the Demon Hypothesis make sense? For an evaluation of the Demon hypothesis see page 41 onwards.
The famous *cogito* argument. Descartes cannot doubt his own existence, as he must exist in order to doubt. The *cogito* is one of the most famous arguments in the history of philosophy, but what sort of argument is it? Is it even an argument at all? And if so does it work? Does it show that an 'I' exists? Perhaps what Descartes thinks is a self is really no more than a series of thoughts. These and other issues relating to the *cogito* are explored from page 47.	I doubt the existence of the physical world, even basic maths, as there may be an evil demon deceiving me.	
	I cannot doubt my existence: I think, I am.	Descartes undertakes some exploratory thoughts on the nature of the 'I'. He tries to work out his essence by considering which parts of him are essential and which are inessential. The only thing he cannot imagine himself without is thought and so he defines himself as a thinking thing. For analysis of this passage see page 63 onwards.
	What sort of thing am I? I am a thinking thing.	

Comment	Central argument	Comment

Comment

Descartes claims the *cogito* works because it is so 'clear' and 'distinct'.

However, how meaningful are these terms? Can Descartes really tell that he knows something for certain just by looking at how clear and distinct his thoughts are? And can he universalise this claim?

These and other criticisms can be found from page 82.

The Cartesian Circle. Descartes has been accused of making a serious error at this point – an error of form not just substance.

Descartes wants to prove that clear and distinct ideas are reliable. In order to do so he proves that God exists, so showing there could be no evil demon deceiving him. But the claim is that his proof relies on clear and distinct ideas. In attempting to show that clear and distinct ideas are always reliable he relies on clear and distinct ideas. The problem is that this approach is circular. For an analysis of the 'Cartesian circle' see pages 98 and 120.

The Ontological Argument. Descartes is claiming that, by analysing the very concept of God, he can prove that God exists.

Is this a trick argument? Does the idea of perfection really entail existence?

For an analysis of the ontological argument see page 113 onwards.

Central argument

It is surprising that I know the nature of myself before that of material objects. But, after considering what I know about wax, I shouldn't really be surprised at all.

I know I exist. This cannot be doubted because it is so clear and distinct.

Anything that is perceived clearly and distinctly must be true.

. . . unless a Demon is deceiving me.

I know that God exists because my idea of an infinite and perfect being must have been caused by one.

I can be certain that anything clearly and distinctly perceived must be true, as God is no deceiver.

Any properties I clearly and distinctly perceive in the idea of God will be properties God has.
God is perfect and existence is part of being perfect, so God must exist.

Comment

Descartes is a bit surprised that his own nature is one of the first certainties he reaches. Before his doubts he felt convinced that he could be more certain about the objects around him than he could be about his own elusive nature. He overcomes this puzzle by considering a piece of wax – suggesting it is the mind, not the senses, that truly understand its nature. The wax cannot be known through the senses as there is no sense datum that remains the same through the various changes undergone by the wax as it melts. So the essence of matter is recognised by the understanding. Also, when he perceives anything he must also be aware of himself. To even perceive the wax requires a human mind. Descartes is now more confident about the way he arrived at an understanding of his own nature.

For criticisms of this passage see page 73 onwards.

Descartes puts forward the 'Trademark' Argument for the existence of God.

How convincing is this? Does anyone really have an idea of a perfect and infinite being? And, if so, must this be caused by one?

For analysis of this argument see page 87 onwards.

Comment

Descartes attempts to establish his dualist thesis. As he can clearly and distinctly conceive of his non-extended mind distinct from his body, he claims it must be a separate substance.

Many critics claim that Descartes is guilty of committing the *masked-man fallacy*. The suggestion is that it is dangerous to argue that because you can think about objects differently they must be different. For an analysis of Descartes' proof and of the *masked-man fallacy* see page 131 onwards.

Central argument

My imagination and sense perceptions involve the ideas of extended bodies (matter). What causes these ideas?

I can conceive of myself clearly and distinctly as a non-extended thing existing distinctly from my body therefore I am distinct from my body.

I cannot be making up the ideas of extended bodies because:
a) I receive sense perceptions passively or against my will and
b) they involve the concept of extension and I am unextended.
As God is no deceiver, my perceptions must be caused by extended objects.

The external world exists but is not exactly how it appears.

Material objects are essentially extended. Extension is a mathematical concept understood by the mind. The world is best understood through the mind not the senses.

God is no deceiver. Everything I conceive clearly and distinctly must be true. The external world exists. The only time I am mistaken is when I make hasty judgements.

Comment

Descartes sets out to prove that the external world exists. In doing so he is overcoming the doubts of *Meditation 1* and discovering the nature of the mind–body relationship.

For an analysis of his argument see page 124 onwards.

Descartes has established that God is no deceiver and that all clear and distinct beliefs must be true. This presents him with the tricky task of accounting for error. Sometimes we appear to be very clear and distinct about something, but yet are still in error – how is this possible if God is no deceiver? Descartes gives the example of amputees who clearly feel that they have an arm when they don't or people who are ill and want to drink even when it is bad for them. In these cases he claims that error occurs because our body is a machine and all machines break down from time to time. He claims that such thoughts are not really clear and distinct so we are not really being deceived by God. See pages 107–8 and page 147.

Immediately after proving that the external world exists, Descartes goes on to say that it is not exactly how it appears. He outlines a primary/secondary quality distinction, suggesting that objects only really have the properties of size, shape, quantity, motion, which we can perceive clearly and distinctly. The properties of colour, sound, taste, smell, etc. are caused by the primary qualities. and are not really properties of the objects themselves.

For a discussion of the primary/secondary quality distinction see page 125 onwards.

Meditation 1: The method of doubt and its application

Descartes' project and the method of doubt

Read *Meditation 1* paragraphs 1 and 2

Page references given as (p. 95) etc. refer to the text of *Meditations*.

Descartes begins the *Meditations* by observing that many of his common-sense opinions have turned out to be false, and that his belief system seems to be full of prejudice and error. Descartes wants to get rid of these errors so as to establish 'something firm and constant in the sciences' (p. 95). In other words he wants to find certainty and durability in human knowledge of the universe and our place in it. To do this he plans first to get rid of all his previous opinions and 'begin afresh from the foundations' (p. 95). By subjecting all his beliefs to DOUBT, he hopes to sweep them away, and so uncover beliefs which can't be doubted. Beliefs which survive any possible doubt must be of the utmost certainty and durability and so are the ideal foundations upon which to rebuild a body of knowledge which will be free from error.

What Descartes is here proposing is to use doubt as a tool to uncover those beliefs which, by surviving scepticism, prove themselves to be beyond any possible doubt, or to be INDUBITABLE. The so-called 'method of doubt' entails suspending judgement about everything he previously took for granted. All that can be doubted is treated as false for the purposes of argument. So Descartes says he doesn't have to prove that any of his previous opinions are false in order to reject them. For the slightest ground for doubt that he finds will be sufficient for him to treat them *as if* they were false. So the burden of proof is on his beliefs to show that they can't be doubted; not on him to show that they must be false. Now, clearly such a standard of proof is very fierce and will lead him to reject very many (if not all!) of his beliefs. But it is precisely because it is so fierce that if anything survives which can't be doubted then this must be absolutely certain. For this reason, the beliefs that survive his radical scepticism should be solid enough to be the foundations upon which he can reconstruct a new body of knowledge free from error. What this means is that Descartes is not himself a sceptic: he does not raise doubts simply for their own sake. Rather his scepticism is a means to an end. He uses sceptical arguments precisely in order to give security to his theory of knowledge by uncovering unshakable first principles.

The last point Descartes makes about his method is that it need not involve going through each of his beliefs in turn and subjecting it to doubt. He has, after all, so many beliefs that this would take him forever. Rather he decides to doubt what he calls the 'principles', i.e. the most fundamental beliefs (p. 96). Since the bulk of his beliefs rest on a few basic principles, by doubting these he can demolish the system more efficiently.

■ Summary of the method of doubt

1 Descartes' project is to eliminate error from his system of beliefs, and establish certain and enduring knowledge.
2 To do this he will destroy all his previous opinions by rejecting any that have the slightest grounds for doubt.
3 He won't go through each belief individually, but will destroy the 'principles' or most basic beliefs, so that the rest will collapse of their own accord.
4 Whatever beliefs survive this method must be indubitable, and so can be the foundations on which to build human knowledge anew free from error.

■ **Figure 4.1 *The method of doubt***

Descartes thinks of his present belief system as like a badly constructed building. It has been built haphazardly on shaky foundations and so is full of errors. To remedy the situation he will demolish the building, find secure foundations, and carefully rebuild so that the new building will be free from error.

Descartes is dismayed that his belief system is so shaky

Descartes, using the bulldozer of doubt, demolishes his old house of beliefs

Descartes reduces all his beliefs to rubble

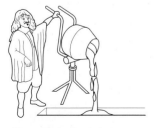

Descartes begins to lay secure foundations

Descartes carefully begins to rebuild a new house of beliefs – one that will last forever

Philosophical doubt and ordinary doubt

Note that the doubt that Descartes is employing here is not like the doubt we are familiar with from our everyday life. Ordinary doubt occurs when you have clear grounds for withholding your assent from some claim; perhaps the source of the claim is questionable, or the nature of it makes it seem unlikely to be true. But Descartes' doubt – sometimes referred to as HYPERBOLIC doubt – is a different kind of doubt altogether. Descartes intends to reject beliefs if he has any grounds *whatsoever* for being suspicious of their truth, not just if he has reasonable grounds.

ACTIVITY   Consider the propositions below. Make a copy of the table. Tick all the boxes that describe your attitude to each proposition.

	A It is not possible for me to doubt this claim.	**B** I have genuine doubts about this claim.	**C** It is theoretically possible for me to doubt this claim.
Humans have landed on the moon.			
Jesus Christ was the son of God.			
Gordon Brown is a politician.			
Shakespeare wrote *Macbeth*.			
I have just read the word 'elephant'.			
The sun will rise tomorrow.			
I am awake.			
Apples do not exist.			
England will win the next football world cup.			
19 is a prime number.			

Column B represents our ordinary, run-of-the-mill doubts. Column C represents philosophical doubt. Hopefully, for every tick in column B you also put a tick in column C, as to doubt a belief *genuinely* implies that it is possible to doubt it *theoretically* . However the reverse is not true. There will be many beliefs that can be theoretically doubted but which, in the ordinary course of life, you hold no genuine doubts about. It is important to remember this distinction when reading the opening *Meditation*, as Descartes is primarily concerned with column C not B. He wants to shake off any beliefs that are even theoretically doubtful, so that he can start building a new system of knowledge based only on doubt-free beliefs. But he does not mean to suggest that he harbours genuine doubts about the beliefs in question. Indeed, if Descartes genuinely doubted most of his beliefs, it is unlikely that he would have bothered to write the *Meditations* at all. For if you genuinely doubted that you were awake, or doubted the very existence of ink, pens or other people, it would certainly make you think twice about putting pen to paper. Philosophical doubt is a useful tool for examining the nature of beliefs, but if genuinely held it would make ordinary life impossible.

The gulf between philosophical doubt and more ordinary mundane concerns is neatly mocked by Woody Allen.

What if everything is an illusion and nothing exists? In that case, I definitely overpaid for my carpet.

Woody Allen, *Without Feathers*, 1976

We need to be clear, however, that Descartes is not saying that his suspension of JUDGEMENT is *merely* an academic exercise which can have no implications for his ordinary beliefs. On the contrary, if he finds good reason to reject his common-sense assumptions, he has resolved to do so. However, in the meantime he cannot genuinely discard all beliefs. For without them he would have nothing to guide his everyday conduct. He would be paralysed, having no reason to do one thing rather than another. While some sceptics might be attracted by such an option, Descartes was not, because, as we have seen, his scepticism is ultimately at the service of his quest for certainty. Consequently he needs a set of rules by which to live until his sceptical meditations are complete. In the *Discourse on Method* Descartes proposes that during this interim he will:

... obey the laws and customs of my country, firmly preserving the religion into which God was good enough to have me instructed from childhood, and governing myself in all other matters according to the most moderate opinions and those furthest from excess, commonly accepted in practice by the most prudent people with whom I should have to live.[9]

In other words, Descartes does not *genuinely* doubt much of the received opinion of his day.

Interpretation and evaluation

■   Is Descartes' doubt sincere?

▶ criticism ◀   These last remarks may raise a worry about the sincerity of Descartes' method. Could it be that the doubts are just a sham, and that Descartes had a pretty good idea of what he wanted to prove from the outset? Or, more generously, isn't there a risk that his prejudices might reassert themselves – even unconsciously – in the process of rebuilding a system of supposedly perfectly indubitable beliefs? If so, we might accuse Descartes of not taking his method seriously enough. For the method to be effective, it may be argued, Descartes needs *genuinely* to destroy all his opinions. A purely theoretical doubt cannot achieve this, since beliefs left in place inevitably prejudice the enquiry. This is certainly the suspicion of many on completing the *Meditations*, for, by the end, the new system of beliefs appears, in most essentials, identical to the system he claimed to demolish. Whether or not you will harbour such suspicions will have to be seen.

■   Can Descartes really doubt all his beliefs?

▶ criticism ◀   There are various serious difficulties with Descartes' pronouncement that he will 'undertake seriously … to rid myself of all the opinions I had adopted up to then' (p. 95). For one, to entertain the possibility that all his opinions could be doubtful invites the question of whether the possibility that all his opinions are doubtful is *itself* doubtful or not. If it *is* then it suggests that not all his beliefs are doubtful after all. But if it is *not* doubtful, then there is at least one opinion that is not doubtful, namely that all his opinions are doubtful. So he can't doubt *this* belief at least, and so not literally *all* his beliefs are doubtful. Either way, it seems, not all of his beliefs can be doubted at once.

In a similar vein consider that if Descartes wants to doubt *all* his beliefs he would have to abandon the belief that he had previous beliefs to doubt. But if he were to doubt *this* it would disable him from doubting any of his other beliefs, since he wouldn't believe he had them. What we are seeing here is that, in order to doubt something, one has to believe at least: that one has beliefs that can be subjected to doubt; that these beliefs can be more or less certain or well justified;

that they may be true or they may be false; that one can raise sceptical difficulties which make them doubtful, and so on. In other words, in order to use sceptical arguments at all, Descartes is bound to take certain assumptions for granted. One needs certain beliefs about the nature of belief, evidence, certainty, truth and so on, in order even to call beliefs into question.

Actually Descartes is not unaware of this fact about the very possibility of doubt. In the *Rules for the Direction of the Mind* he writes:

If Socrates says he doubts everything, it follows necessarily that he knows this at least – that he doubts. Likewise he knows that something can be either true or false, and so on, for all those consequences necessarily attach to the nature of doubt.[10]

What this suggests is that Descartes' scepticism is not really as all encompassing as the opening lines of the *Meditations* suggest. There are limits to how sceptical one can be, and Descartes must retain the basic framework of beliefs concerning the nature of doubt, certainty and evidence which allow his method to operate.

■ Is indubitability too much to ask of our beliefs?

▶ criticism ◀ We may also question another aspect of his method. Is it really reasonable to reject all beliefs about which there is just the slightest doubt? This is a very fierce standard to apply to our beliefs, as we have seen. Surely it would be far more sensible to reject those beliefs about which there is a 'reasonable' doubt, as in a court of law. Think how impractical it would be to demand absolute certainty of our beliefs before we acted. Someone who is overly sceptical never gets anything done since they are always waiting for conclusive evidence. Refusing to believe what is not absolutely certain may ensure that you don't believe anything false, but the down side is that very few beliefs are admitted into your belief system. If, as it may plausibly be argued, we are never going to get conclusive evidence and absolute certainty, then the best option is to accept beliefs which are reasonable given the evidence.

To illustrate the point, suppose Descartes were a defence barrister at a criminal trial at which he asked us, as jury, to adopt his method. Before we could convict he would demand that we establish the defendant's guilt beyond any possible doubt. In such a case, we would have to admit that even though the defendant had the motive; even though his fingerprints were on the gun; and even though a dozen witnesses saw him pull the trigger, it is still *theoretically* possible that he is innocent, say if there were an elaborate conspiracy against him. Even though there is no evidence of any conspiracy, it *is* theoretically possible and so, according to Descartes' standard of proof, we could not convict.

Clearly, if we were to accept Descartes' method in a court of law, we would never convict anyone and this would be extremely impractical. Perhaps, then, things should be the same in philosophy. This is the way the empiricist philosopher David Hume (1711–1776) reasoned in his attack on Descartes' method in his *Enquiry concerning Human Understanding* (1748). 'The Cartesian doubt,' he argued, 'would be entirely incurable; and no reasoning could ever bring us to a state of assurance and conviction upon any subject.'[11] Hume's point is that hyperbolic scepticism, once embarked upon, cannot be escaped since most, or even all, of our beliefs can be doubted *theoretically*. If we begin by demanding so much of our beliefs, we will end up not having very many and so Descartes' method leads us into a sceptical dead end. We will be turning shortly to see how Descartes does try to escape from the scepticism he initiates and then we will be better able to judge whether Hume is right.

■ Why not doubt our beliefs one by one?

► criticism ◄ If we can't reject all our beliefs in one fell swoop, wouldn't a more piecemeal application of the method of doubt be more reasonable? Shouldn't Descartes proceed by criticising his opinions one by one, using other opinions as a basis for doing so? Those that were found to be wanting could then be discarded, and the ones that could not be doubted could be retained. Descartes rejects this approach as too time consuming. He claims that he doesn't need to examine his beliefs one by one because he can question the *principles* upon which they are based. If these principles are found to be doubtworthy, then all the beliefs that are based upon them can be abandoned as well. This way of thinking is really part and parcel of his FOUNDATIONALISM: the view that our system of beliefs is structured like a building with basic beliefs supporting the rest. If this is how our beliefs are structured, then undermining the foundational beliefs will clearly mean those based upon them will collapse also. However, not all philosophers accept foundationalism. Rather than a building, a simile used by anti-foundationalists for our belief system is that of a boat on the open sea. We cannot destroy the boat and rebuild it from scratch, since we would drown; rather we must rebuild it piece by piece. In the same way, it may be that the process of ridding our belief system of error is necessarily a piecemeal affair, since the destruction of all our beliefs leaves us with nothing to operate with. Without beliefs of any sort we cannot function.[12]

Application of the method

Read *Meditation 1*
paragraphs 3–12

Now that we have discussed the method Descartes has elected to use we can turn to his application of the method in *Meditation 1*. Descartes presents us with three distinct sceptical scenarios or 'waves of doubt', each more radical than the last:

1 He doubts the testimony of sense experience by pointing out that it can be deceptive.
2 He doubts the nature of waking life by blurring the distinction with dreaming.
3 He doubts the existence of the physical world and his judgements about simple mathematics by positing the existence of an all-deceiving demon.

Doubting the senses

ACTIVITY
1 Try to think of a situation where your senses deceived you.
2 How did you come to realise that they were deceiving you?
3 Is it possible that the way you came to notice the deception was also a deception?

Read *Meditation 1*
paragraph 3

In the first wave of doubt Descartes argues that because his senses have sometimes deceived him he should no longer trust them for 'it is prudent never to trust entirely those who have once deceived us' (p. 96). The possibility of perceptual error is sufficient to lead him to doubt the whole of sense experience, since his method demands that the slightest doubt about beliefs will lead him to reject them. No example of such deception is given in *Meditation 1*, but in *Meditation 6* Descartes recalls how:

I have observed many times that towers, which from a distance seemed round, appeared at close quarters to be square, and that huge figures erected on the summits of these towers looked like small statues when viewed from below; and thus, in an infinity of other instances, I found error in judgements based on the external senses.
(pp. 154–5)

The possibility of error undermines the principle that one can trust the senses. And if one abandons this principle, as we have seen, all the beliefs that rely upon it will collapse with it. So Descartes doesn't need to question the beliefs about the world obtained through his senses one by one. He doesn't ask 'Is this tower *really* round as it appears?', 'Is this stick *really* bent?', and so on. That would be 'an endless task' as he points out in the second paragraph. Rather, if one doubts that the senses are trustworthy *as such*, the whole edifice of beliefs resting on this foundation stone can be swept aside in one fell swoop.

Interpretation and evaluation

■ Descartes is against empiricism

We see straight away that Descartes' application of his method is directed against the senses. This is because his plan is to undermine empiricism and the view that knowledge comes ultimately from sense experience. What he is trying to do is make us realise that the senses, far from being the most reliable and important source of knowledge, as we might ordinarily think, are in fact the main source of error. It is our unthinking faith in the senses which leads us astray, and so he begins by trying to raise doubts about the senses as the basis for our knowledge of the world.

■ The senses must be trustworthy some of the time

▶ criticism ◀ Another concern philosophers have had with Descartes' first wave of doubt relates to the move he appears to make from saying that his senses are occasionally unreliable to his decision not to trust them at all. For while our senses do *sometimes* deceive us it does not follow that they may *always* deceive us. In fact, we can argue that the only reason we are able to tell that our senses are sometimes deceptive is precisely because on other occasions we take them to be accurate. For example, if I recognise that a stick appears bent when half-immersed in water – but isn't really – this must be because I am able to use my senses to check. I may pull the stick out of the water and look again, or I may immerse my hand to have a feel of its shape. In other words, I use the very same senses to detect the deception. This point is sometimes illustrated through an example of a similar argument which is clearly fallacious. From the fact that some paintings are forgeries, it does not follow that all paintings could be forgeries, in fact quite the contrary. For since a forgery is a copy of a genuine (non-forged) painting, you cannot have forgeries unless you have genuine paintings. If Descartes' argument is indeed of this type then this suggests that it may be self-refuting. To notice that the senses *sometimes* deceive depends on being able to correct errors by appeal to other sensory evidence. Thus the conclusion that the senses might always be deceptive actually relies on the assumption that they are only sometimes deceptive.

However, this objection probably misinterprets Descartes' intention at this stage. Descartes' argument intends to infer from the fact that the senses have deceived us in the past, only that they are not entirely trustworthy and could deceive us again. Thus he is not yet suggesting that the senses might *always* deceive us, but just that we cannot tell when to trust them and when not, and therefore that we should not trust them completely. Descartes is not saying that it is possible every one of his beliefs based upon the senses could be false, but rather that not one of his beliefs based on the senses is guaranteed to be true. This means that each of his beliefs may be false, although not all of them. The key distinction here is between 'possibly all false' – meaning that all of his beliefs may be false (a claim which appears to be incoherent as we saw above) – and 'all possibly false' – which implies that some are true, even though we may not be able to tell which ones. An analogy may help to make Descartes' point. If I know that either the red mushrooms or the green ones are deadly, I have a good reason to abstain from eating both sorts of mushrooms. In the same way Descartes has good reason to withhold assent from all beliefs based on the senses just because he knows some are false, without needing to claim that they could all be false. That this is indeed Descartes' position is supported by his comments in the very next paragraph which state that some of his beliefs based on the senses are surely true, namely those about things which are close at hand, like the fact that he is sitting by the fire.[13]

The Dreaming Argument

ACTIVITY

1 Have you ever had a dream which was so real it felt like real life?

2 Have you ever dreamt you have woken up, got out of bed and got on with your normal life, only to wake up for real later?

3 Have you ever been awake and thought you might be dreaming?

4 How do you know that you're not dreaming now?

Read *Meditation 1* paragraphs 4–7

Descartes now suggests that the previous doubts about the senses only really affect objects at a distance or things which are difficult to perceive properly. We surely can be absolutely certain that we are not being deceived about objects which are right in front of us. Unless, of course, we are mad. However, Descartes now pushes the process of doubt even further to cover even these apparently fundamental perceptual beliefs. For aren't we rather like mad people when in the grip of a dream? When dreaming I have often supposed that I am going about my ordinary daily business, and when in such a dream I am convinced that I am awake. But if I can have dreams which are just like being awake, then I cannot be sure that I am not dreaming now. The sceptical point of the argument is that if I cannot know that I am not now dreaming, any belief I have about what I can perceive around me may be false. So even Descartes' belief that he is sitting by the fire in his dressing gown, a belief which seems so self-evidently true, may not be.

Interpretation and evaluation

■ Dreams can be distinguished from waking life

▶ criticism ◀ Many find this argument unconvincing because they have never had dreams which are at all similar to waking life. Surely, we might think, dreams are very different in character from real life, and so it is relatively easy to tell the difference. And so we might try to mount an objection to Descartes' Dreaming Argument by identifying certain signs or criteria by which we can tell whether or not we are dreaming. For example, we could try pinching ourselves to see whether it hurts, or try to read something; since it is supposed to be impossible to feel pain or to read in a dream.

Descartes anticipates this objection and claims that it misses the point of his argument. For no matter how good I may normally be at distinguishing dreams from waking life, whatever criterion I apply in drawing the distinction, whatever test I use to tell that I am awake, it remains possible that I merely *dream* that the criterion is satisfied or the test passed. For I could always *dream* that I pinch myself and that it hurts, or *dream* that I can read the words on the page in front of me. That is, I could always dream that this experience I am having has all the hallmarks of waking life. Descartes concludes that there can be no 'conclusive signs by means of which one can distinguish clearly between being awake and being asleep' (p. 97).

■ Dreams must come from waking life

▶ criticism ◀ Similar objections to those against the argument for perceptual illusion have often been levelled against Descartes' Dreaming Argument too. For example, it might be pointed out that from the fact that I am *sometimes* unaware that I am dreaming, it doesn't follow I might *always* be unaware that I am dreaming. Also one might point out that the concept of a dream is that of a kind of copy of waking life. And so, as with the forged painting example above, to be able to say that one has had dreams which are just like waking life presupposes that there is a distinction between the two. If all life were a dream, then there would be no contrast with waking life on which the very concept of a dream depends, and so it would make no sense to call it a 'dream'.

▶ criticism ◀ A similar approach begins by noting that the contents of my dreams ultimately come from waking life, in the sense that what I dream about is not totally made up but composed out of memories of real-life experiences. So while I might dream about flying on a carpet, such a fantasy is nonetheless based in reality: I have after all experienced carpets and seen things fly when awake. It follows from this that if I am dreaming then I must have been awake at some point, otherwise I would have nothing to be dreaming about.

▶ criticism ◀ In the same vein, against the claim that I might always be dreaming, it can be pointed out that in ordinary language we are perfectly able to distinguish dreaming from waking. Such terms only gain currency by being used in a fairly consistent way. Now, if I were always dreaming I should not be able to distinguish dreaming from waking and so one of the terms would be redundant. For 'dreaming' to have any reference there must be a state with which to contrast it. Therefore I can know that I am not always dreaming.

However, while such arguments might show that I am not *always* dreaming, they don't show that I am not dreaming *now*. And it is doubtful that Descartes actually wants to claim at this stage that he might always be dreaming. To question whether I am dreaming now may raise enough doubts about the VERACITY (i.e. truthfulness or accuracy) of sensation for his present purposes. This interpretation is given support by the fact that Descartes suggests that the Dreaming Argument does not raise doubts about the existence of physical objects *as such*. For the most basic constituents from which our dreams are made are not themselves mere figments of our sleeping life, among which he lists 'corporeal nature in general [i.e. physical things] and its extension; the shape of extended objects; quantity, or the size and number of these objects; place for them to exist in, and time for them to endure through; and so on' (p. 98).

■ You can't know you've had dreams indistinguishable from waking life

▶ criticism ◀ The feeling that Descartes' argument may be self-refuting, however, may persist. Can Descartes even use the premise that he sometimes has dreams which are indistinguishable from waking life? How could he ever know this? For, on the one hand, to know this premise to be true is to know such dreams to be indistinguishable. And yet if you *know* you have had such dreams, they *must* be distinguishable (otherwise you wouldn't know you'd had them). So, paradoxically, you cannot know the truth of the claim to know that you have had dreams which are indistinguishable unless it is false.

However, this objection doesn't show that the premise actually *is* false; only that one cannot know that it is true. But Descartes doesn't need to *know* the premise for his doubts to get going. Simply believing, or even entertaining the possibility, that he may have had dreams which were indistinguishable from waking life may be enough to raise doubts about whether he might be dreaming now. Moreover, Descartes' argument relies only on the premise that he has had dreams which are indistinguishable from waking life *while he was having them*. They may well have become distinguishable upon awaking. For this premise can raise the doubts he needs: namely that he might be dreaming *now*, even though this dream may well be identified as such when he wakes.

In keeping with the interpretation that Descartes is not suggesting that he might always be dreaming, Descartes' next paragraph (6) points out that, even if he is dreaming, there must be a real world out there from which he has got the materials to compose his dream. A dreamer is like a painter who makes up the creatures populating his or her landscape, but the basic colours and shapes are still originally gained from real life. This suggests that, whether or not I am dreaming, some very general truths about the world must be knowable: perhaps that it is coloured, and has spatial dimensions. Pushing this line of thought further (paragraph 7), Descartes figures that, whether or not his present experiences are real, the basic truths of mathematics and of geometry remain true. 'For whether I am awake or sleeping, two and three added together always make five, and a square never has more than four sides; and it does not seem possible that truths so apparent can be suspected of any falsity or uncertainty' (p. 98). I can see that these claims are true regardless of whether I am awake or asleep.

The evil demon

Read *Meditation 1* paragraphs 8–11

Even with mathematical truths there may be room for doubt. I have, after all, made mistakes in arithmetic before. Could it be that I am mistaken now, even in things that seem as obvious as that 2 + 3 = 5? Could I go wrong when counting the sides of a square, so that what seem to be four sides might really be three or five? We experience no difference between believing the right and believing the wrong answer to a sum; so if there were an all-powerful God he would be able to deceive me into thinking I was right when I was in fact wrong. Descartes' point here seems to be that while mathematical truths are knowable A PRIORI – that is to say, simply by thinking about them regardless of any knowledge we have gained through experience – nonetheless we are prone to error about them. And if it is always possible for us to be mistaken in our judgements, then we can always doubt their veracity.

However, Descartes continues, my idea of God is of a being which is not only OMNIPOTENT, but supremely good. And for him to deceive me in this way about simple mathematics would surely be inconsistent with such goodness. And yet it would seem to be no less inconsistent with his goodness for him to deceive me about other things I used to take to be obvious, and yet I clearly *am* deceived in some such things, as has been shown.

These considerations lead Descartes to abandon the notion of a deceiver God. After all, it may be that no God exists. Indeed, it is possible that there is an extremely powerful and malicious demon who employs all his energies to deceive us. Descartes imagines that such a demon would be powerful enough to deceive him about the very existence of the physical world. The appearance to him of the sky and the earth, of colours, shapes and sounds, may all be illusions. Even the appearance of his own body may be part of the demon's deception. With this final and most radical wave of doubt the first *Meditation* concludes. In the metaphor which opens the second, the deep water of doubt is all-engulfing and bottomless – until Descartes manages to find his first firm foothold: namely the proposition 'I exist'. It is from this that the positive rebuilding phase of the epistemological enterprise begins.

ACTIVITY In the film *The Matrix* the hero, Neo, lives in a world very much like this one, where he goes to work, goes home, gets on with life, etc. However, early in the film, Neo makes a terrifying discovery. The world he inhabits isn't real, it is part of 'the matrix', a computer-generated simulation world. Neo takes a pill to remove him from the computer simulation and wakes up to find that he has cables going into his spine that had been feeding him false information to his brain and making him believe that he had a home, a job, etc. Neo pulls the cables out and sees the world as it really is – a world controlled by computers who have enslaved human beings.

1 Do you think that this scenario is a possibility? Is it possible that the world in front of you now isn't the real world, but is just being 'implanted' into your head?

2 How do you know that you're not in 'the matrix' at this very minute?

3 How does Neo know (when he 'wakes up' and pulls the cables out of his spine) that this new world (i.e. the one where he sees computers enslaving human beings) isn't also an illusion?

▨ Brain in a vat

A more recent version of Descartes' Evil Demon Argument is the thought experiment known as the 'brain in a vat'. A version of this might run as follows:

Imagine the year is now 2720. Somewhere in a laboratory a mad scientist is undertaking an evil experiment. He has placed a human brain in a vat of chemicals. Connected to the brain are thousands of wires which carry electro-chemical signals to and fro between the brain and a vast computer. The scientist is feeding images, sounds, noises and sensations to the brain to make the brain think it is in fact a person living at the beginning of the twenty-first century. The brain even thinks that at this precise moment it is a person reading a philosophy book on Descartes.

▨ **Figure 4.2**
Brain in a vat of chemicals

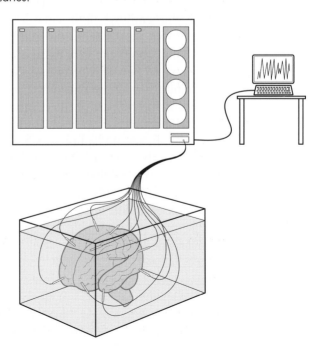

Is this a possibility? If so, could *you* really be a brain in a vat? Even if this is only 0.00001 per cent likely, if you accept that it is theoretically possible doesn't that mean that you can never be 100 per cent certain of anything?

You may be tempted to think that one way or another at least you have a brain and that the earth still exists even if you are in a vat being controlled by an evil computer. But even these thoughts are not certain. The world as you know it might only be the creation of the scientist, and the very idea of a brain might be simply another illusion that has been fed to you by the scientist. You could be anything in that vat: some kind of slug, a cloud or something totally unimaginable. Once the scenario is established, the possibility for doubt seems endless. Is there anything you could be certain of?

ACTIVITY   Look again at the list of propositions on page 30 of this book. In the light of Descartes' Evil Demon Argument or the *Matrix* or 'Brain in a vat' scenarios, ask yourself whether any of the propositions are free from doubt.

Interpretation and evaluation

■ Doubting reason is self-defeating

It seems that Descartes is saying that the Dreaming Argument is limited in that it cannot throw doubt on *a priori* knowledge, or on the existence of the most fundamental units of our waking experience, namely the existence of shape or extension, sounds, colours, etc. Only a deceiving God or an evil demon can call these truths into question too. Thus the third wave of sceptical reasoning is presented as a reason for doubting even these minimal beliefs about real existence and about the most basic mathematics.

▶ criticism ◀   However, the doubts about his basic mathematical judgements lead to an important difficulty for Descartes to which we will be returning. If the demon hypothesis can cast doubt on such simple reasoning processes as are involved in counting the sides of a square and adding 2 to 3, it should also cast doubt on our capacity to make basic logical inferences, such as the inference that a supremely good God would not deceive us about mathematics and geometry. So if the demon could be fooling me into thinking that $2 + 3 = 5$, when it does not, surely he might also be fooling me into thinking that God would not deceive me, when he would. As we shall see, the idea that God would not deceive us about such basic reasoning processes is crucial to the development of Descartes' argument, but the point runs deeper than this. For if I cannot trust my basic reasoning processes then I must give up my belief in argument as a means of acquiring the truth. If the reliability of reason is doubted then how can Descartes hope to use reason to overcome his doubt? It seems that, in pushing his scepticism thus far, his whole enterprise must grind to a halt.

So, while Descartes can engage in doubt about a particular domain, namely what the senses teach, he cannot seriously doubt the possibility of rational thought itself, since he has to use reason to do so. As we saw above, there is a basic logic to the very use of the concept of doubt such that, in order meaningfully to doubt one thing, something else needs to be taken as certain. In other words, at the very least, the possibility of doubt is premised on the distinction between truth and falsehood. If I can doubt something I must know what it means to say that a belief may be true or false.

◾ The Evil Demon Hypothesis is empty

▶ criticism ◀

Critics have complained that the supposition of an evil demon deceiving me about the existence of the physical world is empty if the demon's trickery is undetectable. The idea here is that if I could never tell the difference *even in principle* between the demon's deceiving me and my having a veridical experience, then for all practical purposes there is no difference. It is, as it were, a difference which makes no difference, since there are no criteria (or at least none available to me) for drawing the distinction between deception and reality. To illustrate the point, consider the idea of a counterfeit ten pound note which is so perfect, that it is impossible to tell it from the real thing. No conceivable test would ever be able to detect anything to indicate that it was anything other than a genuine note. This would be a case of a perfect deception. But if the deception is this perfect – so perfect that it cannot be detected even in principle – then surely it is no different from a real note. Certainly, one would have no trouble using the note and it would pass unnoticed into circulation like all other notes, and, the thought goes, there is no real sense in which a fake which does all that the real thing does can meaningfully be called a fake. An undetectable counterfeit is effectively the same as a genuine note. In the same way, if Descartes' demon is able to produce a perfect illusion, one which we can never detect, then surely it is identical with what we call reality.

It's worth pausing to draw parallels here between Descartes' Evil Demon Argument and the recent *Matrix* films (mentioned in the activity above) in which late twentieth-century reality is an illusion generated by a race of machines which have in fact enslaved humanity. In this case, there is a way of detecting the difference between the illusion and reality. It is possible to escape the illusion, as the heroes of the films do, in order to wage war with the machines in their efforts to liberate humanity. And things are similar in *The Truman Show* (1998) in which the Jim Carrey character, Truman Burbank – unbeknown to him – has been a soap opera character all his life. The lake-bound island where he lives is actually a film set, and his friends and family merely actors. But he is able to detect the deception by finally sailing across the lake and touching the painted wooden sky. In these scenarios the deception is meaningful because those deceived can – at least in principle – expose the illusion for what it is. But if, as seems to be the case, Descartes' demon is so cunning that no such discovery is possible, then it is surely an empty hypothesis.

Key points: Chapter 4

What you need to know about *Meditation 1* – the method of doubt and its application:

1 Descartes' project is to establish enduring knowledge in the sciences and to do this he begins by subjecting all his previous opinions to doubt. He resolves to withhold assent from any that are even slightly doubtful.
2 Descartes will not need to go through each of his beliefs one by one, since he can doubt the principles on which they rest. In this way he can destroy his belief system more efficiently.
3 Any beliefs that can survive Descartes' hyperbolic scepticism must be impossible to doubt, and so are good candidates on which to rebuild a body of knowledge free from error.
4 Descartes uses three main sceptical arguments to undermine his current belief system, doubting the senses, the dreaming argument and the evil demon hypothesis. The first involves raising doubts about the reliability of the senses. If his senses can be deceptive then he should not trust them.
5 But even though the senses are sometimes deceptive, they surely cannot deceive him about those things that appear most evident, such as that he is sitting by the fire in his dressing gown. And yet Descartes recalls that he has had dreams in which he has supposed himself to be precisely in this position, when in reality he was naked in his bed. This

suggests that he could be dreaming now and so he cannot know that anything around him is real.

6 However, even if Descartes is dreaming, surely some very basic and general things can be known about reality, since dreams must obtain their materials from waking life. These might include the existence of matter, space and time. Moreover, it seems that the truths of maths and geometry can still be known whether he is awake or asleep.

7 However, Descartes recalls that he had believed in the existence of an all-powerful being, God, who would be able to deceive him about anything. So if such a being does exist, he might be deceiving Descartes about the very existence of the world, and even about his basic judgements of maths and geometry.

8 Descartes' idea of God, however, is that of a perfectly good being, and such deception would seem to be inconsistent with his goodness. So Descartes elects to suppose that the deceiver might be a powerful demon instead. This is the most radical sceptical scenario. It implies that there may not be any physical universe, even his own body may be part of the illusion, and that basic judgements cannot be relied upon. If Descartes can defeat this doubt, he will be certain of having found a piece of truly indubitable knowledge.

5

Meditation 2: The cogito and the nature of the mind

The cogito

Read Meditation 2 paragraphs 1–4

ACTIVITY   Think through Descartes' sceptical arguments again, but this time try to put yourself in his shoes so that you are really doubting everything for yourself.

1 Can you really imagine that your senses are deceiving you? What difficulties does this idea raise?

2 Can you really imagine that you are living in a dream? What difficulties does this idea raise?

3 Can you really imagine that you are a brain in a vat, or that you are being deceived by an all-powerful demon? What difficulties does this idea raise?

4 Describe what it would be like if the Evil Demon Scenario were true. How would you react to the discovery that the familiar world, your friends and family, didn't really exist?

5 Finally try to imagine that even you, yourself, don't exist. What difficulties does this idea raise?

In the search for something certain Descartes has been left, it seems, with nothing. His body, the world, basic maths and God have all fallen foul of his radical scepticism. In the second *Meditation* he presses his doubt still further and wonders if he could even be deceived about his own existence. Maybe he too doesn't exist! But, he reasons, if he is being deceived then he must exist. The all-powerful demon cannot deceive *nothing* into thinking that it exists when it doesn't. And so at the time of thinking that he is something, Descartes cannot in fact be nothing. Thus whenever he conceives the proposition 'I am, I exist' at that moment it is certain to be true.

ACTIVITY   Read through paragraph 4 of *Meditation 2*. Try to reconstruct the ARGUMENT above by identifying and numbering the PREMISES and arriving at the CONCLUSION that 'it is certain that I exist'.

At last Descartes has discovered the first principle that he has been searching for – what is often termed the COGITO – after the formulations of other works of his (namely the *Discourse on Method* and *The Principles of Philosophy*): I am thinking therefore I exist, or, in Latin, *cogito ergo sum*. It is the Archimedean point which enables his epistemological enterprise to make some headway in the sea of doubts into which he has plunged. For just as Archimedes (*c*.287BC–212BC), the great mathematician and scientist of antiquity, claimed that, if given a long enough lever and a fixed fulcrum on which to turn it, he could move the whole earth, so too Descartes hopes that by starting with this one certainty he will be able to discover others and ultimately rebuild his system of knowledge.

Interpretation and evaluation

Difficulties of interpretation

Descartes' apparent discovery of his own existence has been one of the most analysed pronouncements in the history of philosophy. Over the years this deceptively simple claim has caused an enormous amount of controversy and argument. One of the key difficulties in evaluating the *cogito* lies in trying to establish just what sort of a claim it is in the first place. For while it is intuitively convincing for many, articulating exactly how it works is not as simple as it seems. Below we consider different answers to the question of how it might work.

Is the *cogito* an inference?

An inference is the move we make when reasoning from premises to a conclusion. Any argument involves such a move. For example, the argument *Descartes was a great mathematician, therefore he must have been great at one thing at least* provides us with one premise, that *Descartes was a great mathematician*, and infers the conclusion that *he must have been great at one thing at least*. Now, a preliminary answer to our question about the *cogito* is that it too might be an argument of this sort involving an inference from the premise that *I am thinking* to the conclusion that *I exist*. This interpretation is certainly suggested by the 'therefore' of the *Discourse* and *Principles* versions of the *cogito*. However, an inference from the premise that *I am thinking* to the conclusion that *I exist* would not be valid as it stands since we cannot introduce information into the conclusion of an argument – in this case existence – that was not already in the premises. In other words, the conclusion is not fully supported by the premise because it concludes more than can legitimately be inferred from the information given. To see this, consider the following example of an argument which has the same form as this interpretation of Descartes' *cogito*:

I am reading, therefore I must be wearing my glasses.

Now, this may well be a valid inference for me to make, but not as it stands. For the fact that I am reading, *on its own*, is not enough to conclude that I must be wearing glasses, because I may not need glasses to read. For the conclusion to follow we need to assume that I cannot read without my glasses, or that I need my glasses to read. So the complete argument must include this hidden premise:

I am reading.
I need to wear my glasses to read.
Therefore, I am wearing my glasses.

So if we are to take the *cogito* to be an argument of this form then we are going to have to add the hidden premise, which would be something to the effect that *I cannot think without existing*, or *to think one must exist*, or something more general still such as *all thinking things exist*. So a complete version of the argument would run:

I am thinking.
To think one must exist.
Therefore I exist.

So if Descartes did intend the *cogito* to be an inference then he would have to be making implicit appeal to this hidden premise since nowhere does he mention it. Does this mean he thinks it is so self-evident that it does not need to be explicitly stated? Possibly. However, we should recall here that Descartes' method requires him to doubt all his beliefs, and he has not proved that *to think one must exist* or that *all thinking things exist*. How could he have come by such knowledge? Certainly not through his past experience since, we must remember, he is doubting the very existence of the universe, including any thinking things he may have come across in his life. In any case it would be peculiar if at the stage where Descartes is as yet unsure of his *own* existence he could be sure of the general claim that all thinking things exist. So it would surely be illegitimate for him to assume that they do.

Moreover this interpretation of the *cogito* runs into textual difficulties, as Descartes explicitly states in the *Second Replies*: 'When someone says "I am thinking therefore I am, or I exist", he does not deduce existence from thought by means of a SYLLOGISM but recognises it as something self-evident by a simple intuition of the mind.'[14]

And there is another difficulty facing the interpretation of the *cogito* as an inference. Note that the 'I', the existence of which Descartes is claiming to establish in the conclusion of the argument, actually makes an appearance in the premise when he claims: *I think*. This suggests that he has already assumed the existence of himself at the outset, in which case there can be no question of his inferring that he exists. So it seems that the *cogito* argument cannot involve a traditional form of inference.

Is the *cogito* analytically true?

A second possibility, and one suggested by the comment that one can recognise one's existence through the *cogito* by a 'simple intuition of the mind', is that Descartes regards the *cogito* as an *analytic* truth; that is to say, as true simply in virtue of the meanings of the terms used. In other words, Descartes' claim would be that the concept of my present existence is *contained within* that of my thinking, much as the concept of 'female fox' is contained within that of 'vixen'. Just as I can know that *all vixens are foxes* just by analysing the meaning of word 'vixen', so too can I know that I exist just by analysing the meaning of the premise that *I am thinking*. The *cogito* would therefore be not an inference but an identity statement known to be true by pure conceptual analysis. It would not have to make reference to any additional and unproven premises, but could be known *a priori*.

But this interpretation also runs into difficulties, for while the *cogito* might well be thought indubitable because knowable purely *a priori*, it would also be empty of EMPIRICAL content. This is because analytic propositions are normally thought to tell us only about the meanings of terms and the relations between them and nothing about what does or does not exist. They tell us about our *concepts*, but not about *reality*. If the *cogito* were truly analytic nothing substantial about the world could follow from it and so it could not serve as the foundation for knowledge about the world and what exists in it.

Moreover the notion that the concept of a thinking thing entails that of its own existence is surely as absurd as to say that the concept of a vixen entails the concept of its existence. For we can meaningfully talk of thinking things going out of existence just as we can talk of vixens becoming extinct. Existence, we might say, is not a property among other properties that things have, but rather the condition of possibility for having properties at all and so it cannot be part of the concept of any thing, be it thinking or otherwise, that

more
difficult

it exist. To see this, consider the case of fictional characters. Clearly it makes sense to talk about Homer Simpson having thoughts. And we would like to say that we can truly ascribe certain thoughts to him and not others. We can even imagine Homer performing the *cogito*. But we would also want to say that he doesn't really exist. And similarly with Descartes himself: we can say that Descartes no longer exists, even though he truly said 'I think: I exist'. This suggests that we can meaningfully talk of non-existent thinkers, in a way that we cannot speak of married bachelors, or non-female vixens and therefore that there is no relation of *conceptual* entailment between existence and thought.

We can finally dismiss this interpretation based on a careful reading of the text of *Meditation* 2. Descartes writes revealingly that '*I am, I exist*, is necessarily true, every time I express it or conceive of it in my mind' (p. 103). Here he is pointing out that what makes the *cogito* known is the actual process of thinking it through for oneself. In other words, he cannot be saying that the *cogito* is a logical identity true in all possible states of affairs, since knowledge of his existence depends on his conceiving it. So the *cogito* is not really a truth about concepts but a truth about the person conceiving the concepts.

Is the *cogito* a transcendental argument?

A third possibility is that the *cogito* is a TRANSCENDENTAL ARGUMENT. To explain what such an argument is, consider the following line of reasoning. It might be the case that certain things must be true in order for you meaningfully to doubt anything at all. Perhaps your existence is one of these things. If this is the case then it would be impossible to doubt that you exist, as existence is a necessary condition for doubt to occur in the first place. So the very act of doubting actually proves that you exist and the attempt to doubt your own existence becomes self-defeating.

Arguments such as the one above are called *transcendental* arguments (a term first used after Descartes by the great German philosopher Immanuel Kant, 1724–1804). Such arguments 'transcend' the possibility of doubt by suggesting that certain things must be true in order for doubt to exist, in other words by highlighting the PRECONDITIONS of doubt. These preconditions are then impossible to doubt, as the very act of doubting means that they must be true. The generic form of a transcendental argument to defeat scepticism would be something like this:

If *x* is a precondition of doubt then it is impossible to doubt *x*.

Consider the following items and ask yourself which of them would have to exist or be in place in order for doubt to happen. In other words, which of these are preconditions of doubting?

1 The capacity to use language
2 Free will
3 Self-awareness
4 The existence of French wine
5 A mind
6 The ability to reason reliably
7 Time
8 A reliable memory
9 The physical world
10 Reliable perceptions about the physical world.

Here is a possible line of thought about the first of these. If I were unable to use language, how would I develop an argument in order to express doubts about anything? If I am to doubt something, surely I have to be able to say something like 'I doubt my senses are reliable because they have deceived me in the past'. But in the act of formulating such doubts I am using language. So it seems that any sceptic must accept that they can at least use language. Any attempt to doubt this would appear to defeat itself as soon as it was expressed. The sceptic might respond to this by arguing that it is possible to *think* without having a language. So, whether or not I had learned to talk, it is still possible to think thoughts such as 'I doubt that I am awake'. The issue here hinges on how central you take language to be to the possibility of thought.

So when Descartes puts forward the *cogito* is he intending it to be a transcendental argument? In *Meditation 2*, just preceding the '*I am, I exist*' claim, Descartes raises the evil demon possibility once again:

But there is some deceiver, both very powerful and very cunning, who constantly uses all his wiles to deceive me. There is therefore no doubt that I exist, if he deceives me; and let him deceive me as much as he likes, he can never cause me to be nothing, so long as I think I am something. (p. 103)

This could be interpreted as suggesting that Descartes believes that the act of deception somehow implies his existence; that if he is being deceived this shows that he must exist, since the demon cannot deceive nothing into thinking it is something.

This interpretation is backed up by the text of the *Discourse*:

I decided to feign that everything that had entered my mind hitherto was no more true than the illusions of dreams. But immediately upon this I noticed that while I was trying to think everything false, it must needs be that I, who was thinking this, was something.[15]

Here again, the certainty of his existence seems to be drawn from the act of doubting itself, suggesting that, in order to doubt, one must exist.

However, as we consider below, his confidence that he exists might not stem just from the fact that he is being deceived or from doubting *per se*, but rather from the fact that he is *thinking*, of which being deceived and doubting are specific examples. Indeed, if Descartes had thought that his existence could be proved precisely because it was a precondition of doubt, then why didn't he write 'I doubt, therefore I am'?

It is also unlikely that a transcendental argument could deliver the sort of proof that Descartes requires at this stage of the *Meditations*. Before the *cogito*, Descartes is racked with all manner of doubts, as the idea of an evil demon deceiving him renders all his beliefs potentially false. But, although he doesn't discuss the point in *Meditation 1*, such hyperbolic doubt must surely also undermine any confidence he might have in the reliability of his memory. For a demon powerful enough to deceive Descartes about the existence of the physical universe could also deceive him about the past and could have fabricated Descartes' memories. Indeed, the demon may have created Descartes just one second ago, but with a full set of false memories and so Descartes cannot rely on his memory over even the shortest period of time. And yet, a fairly complex transcendental argument, such as the one outlined above, would need to be constructed in the mind over a period of time, probably at least a few seconds, and thus would seem to require a reliable memory. But if Descartes, as yet, cannot trust his memory, it seems that this cannot be the argument that Descartes intended. If the c*ogito* is to work it would seem to have to work in a single moment, as a single and indivisible thought. Only in this way, freed from relying on memory, could Descartes be instantly persuaded of its truth.

Is the *cogito* a self-verifying thought?

This leads us to a fourth possibility: that the *cogito* is a SELF-VERIFYING thought. As we have seen, Descartes emphasises the temporary and fleeting nature of the *cogito* when he writes that, '*I am, I exist*, is necessarily true, every time I express it or conceive of it in my mind' (p. 103). The emphasis here is on the truth of the *cogito* being made apparent through the act of performing it. And this fits with the point made above that the *cogito* cannot rely on a long series of argued steps as an evil demon may be playing with Descartes' mind. Perhaps then Descartes is saying that his existence is a precondition not just of doubting but of doing anything at all. On this reading, the *cogito* would be saying that in order to think, or breathe, or do anything else, I first must exist. And since I am sure that I am thinking, I can be sure that I exist.

This, however, can't be quite right since Descartes clearly believes that the fact that he derives existence from his *thinking* is of paramount significance. He argues in the *Replies* that other ways of reaching the conclusion that I exist will not do. For example, I cannot prove my existence by saying 'I am breathing therefore I exist', even though it would seem equally clear that if I am breathing I must exist. The reason for this is that this premise makes reference to the existence of my body – to my lungs, throat, and so on – and so is subject to doubt since Descartes has not yet proved that he has a body. Only a premise which refers to an act of *thinking* will have the property of having its truth confirmed by the very act of doubting it. For, as outlined above, I cannot doubt that I am doubting since in the very attempt I refute myself. This is because doubting is itself a case of thinking, and just as one cannot doubt that one is doubting, one cannot doubt that one is thinking. So the truth of the *cogito* is verified through the act of thinking it. It is the very act of thinking it which makes it true.

This is not the same as saying the *cogito* is true by definition. We can see this by considering a denial of the *cogito*. The propositions 'I am not thinking' and 'I do not exist' are not false *by definition*, since I may well not have existed. Rather they are made false by being entertained or thought by the person in question. Much like writing 'I am not writing' would be made false in the very act of writing, or saying 'I am not talking' cannot be said truly. When actually uttered or written by someone such propositions become pragmatically self-defeating or self-falsifying. On the other hand, it is impossible to say 'I am talking' or to write 'I am writing' without these propositions being true while you are producing them, and only while producing them. It is in this same manner that we can see that the truth of the *cogito* is self-verifying or self-confirming: it must be true so long as you are thinking it, since thinking it makes it true.

It is important to note in this regard that Descartes' formulation of the *cogito* in the *Meditations* implies (at least initially) that we may cease to exist while we are not thinking. Consequently, at this stage the existence of the self has a rather provisional and temporary character. The task which still faces Descartes is to transform this isolated act of cognition into the basis for a solid system of knowledge.

■ Philosophers' criticisms of the *cogito*

Having devoted some considerable time to our interpretation of this crucial step on Descartes' journey we can now turn to the important issue of evaluating it. To help with this, the exercise below asks you to consider a series of critical thoughts on Descartes' *cogito* made by famous philosophers.

The major claims that Descartes makes on the basis of the *cogito* argument are summed up in this passage from the *Discourse on Method*.

> *Then, examining attentively what I was, and seeing that I could pretend that I had no body and that there was no world or place that I was in, but that I could not, for all that, pretend that I did not exist, ... I thereby concluded that I was a substance, of which the whole essence or nature consists of thinking, and which, in order to exist, needs no place and depends on no material thing; so that this 'I', that is to say, the mind, by which I am what I am, is entirely distinct from the body. (Discourse on Method 4)*

The main claims seem to be:

■ Although I can doubt the existence of my body, I cannot doubt the existence of my *self*.
■ So I must be a SUBSTANCE.
■ The essence of this substance is *thinking*.
■ I can exist independently of material things such as my body.

However, not all philosophers have been persuaded that he can go as far as this. Overleaf is a series of well-known comments on the *cogito* made over the past three hundred years.

1 Read through each quotation (overleaf) in turn and see if you can work out what objection is being made.
2 Ask yourself how you think Descartes might defend his position.
3 Finally consider whether you think the objection has a valid point. Who is right?

► criticism ◄ **1** In search of something certain, at the beginning of *Meditation 2* Descartes attempts to push his doubt still further. If it is conceivable that he is deceived about the existence of the external world, could he also be deceived about his *own* existence? He concludes that he cannot for the proposition 'I am, I exist' cannot be doubted. For if he is thinking, it is self-evident that he must exist. Pierre Gassendi, commenting on the manuscript of the *Meditations*, is puzzled by Descartes' proof. His and others' *Objections* were published with the first edition of the *Meditations*.

But I don't see that you needed all this mechanism, when you had other grounds for being sure ... that you existed. You might have inferred that from any other activity, since our natural light informs us that whatever acts also exists.[16]

► criticism ◄ **2** Descartes claims that the *cogito* establishes the existence of his *self* or *I*. Bertrand Russell believes that the *cogito* establishes far less even than this.

But some care is needed in using Descartes' argument. 'I think, therefore, I am' says rather more than is strictly certain. It might seem as though we were quite sure of being the same person today as we were yesterday ... But the real Self is ... hard to arrive at ... and does not seem to have that absolute, convincing certainty that belongs to particular experiences. When I look at my table and see a certain brown colour, what is quite certain at once is not 'I am seeing a brown colour'; but rather, 'a brown colour is being seen'. This of course involves something (or somebody) which (or who) sees the brown colour; but it does not of itself involve that more or less permanent person whom we call 'I'. So far as immediate certainty goes, it might be that the something which sees the brown colour is quite momentary, and not the same as the something which has some different experience the next moment.[17]

► criticism ◄ **3** In a famous passage opposing Descartes, Hume claims that he has no consciousness of himself.

There are some philosophers who imagine we are every moment intimately conscious of what we call our self; that we feel its existence and its continuance in existence .... For my part, when I enter most intimately into what I call myself I always stumble on some particular perception or other, heat or cold, light or shade, love or hatred, pain or pleasure. I never can catch myself at any time without a perception, and never can observe anything but the perception.[18]

▶ criticism ◀ **4** Georg Lichtenberg, the eighteenth-century German physicist and aphorist, also raised famous doubts about the *cogito*.

'It thinks', we really ought to say, just as we say, 'It thunders'. To say cogito *is too much, if we translate this as 'I think'.*

▶ criticism ◀ **5** Through the *cogito* Descartes claims that he is immediately aware of the self which is the SUBJECT of all his experiences as distinct from the experiences themselves. Again not all philosophers have been persuaded. In a famous passage from his *Tractatus* Wittgenstein argues that there is no such thing as the subject of experience.

There is no such thing as the subject that thinks or entertains ideas. … The subject does not belong to the world: rather, it is a limit of the world. Where in the world is a metaphysical subject to be found? You will say that this is exactly like the case of the eye and the visual field. But really you do not see the eye. And nothing in the visual field allows you to infer that it is seen by an eye. For the form of the visual field is surely not like this:[19]

■ **Figure 5.1**
This picture of the eye and its visual field is incorrect. The eye cannot be inside its own visual field, in other words it cannot see itself

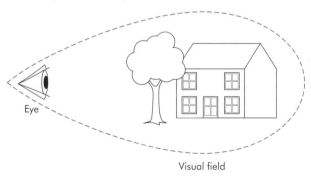

Eye

Visual field

▶ criticism ◀ **6** By the end of the *Meditations* Descartes will claim that he has shown that the mind discovered through the *cogito* is something IMMATERIAL: a thinking substance which is distinct from the body. Mersenne, however, writing in the *Objections,* asks us to pause and take a closer look at Descartes' argument.

*Up to this point you know that you are a being that thinks;
but you do not know what this thinking thing is. What if that
were a body which by its various motions and encounters
produces that which we call thought? ... For how will you prove
that a body cannot think, or that its bodily motions are not
thought itself? Possibly even, the whole bodily system, which
you imagine you have rejected, or some of its parts, say the
parts composing the brain, can unite to produce these motions
which we call thoughts. 'I am a thinking thing,' you say; but
who knows but you are a corporeal motion, or a body in
motion?[20]*

■ Feedback from Activity

Did you manage to decipher what each philosopher was
saying? Let's look at each quotation in turn.

Criticism 1 Gassendi's point appears to be that in order to
do anything I must first exist. So if I am breathing, or
running, or talking, then I must exist, just as clearly as if I am
thinking. So Descartes had no need to produce such a
complex argument to prove his existence and rely on the fact
that he is thinking, since he could have proved he existed
from anything he happened to be doing.

Descartes would respond that Gassendi is missing the
point. For the whole thrust of his argument is that the only
thing he can be sure of doing is thinking, since all other
activities depend on the existence of his body, which is open
to doubt. So while it may well be true that he must exist *if* he
is breathing, since he cannot know that he really *is* breathing
he cannot use this as the starting point of his argument.

Criticism 2 Russell's thought is that in performing the *cogito*
the thing we prove the existence of is not the same thing as
the person we use the word 'I' to refer to. So I cannot by the
cogito argument prove the existence of the person who was
born on a certain date, to certain parents, and has lived a
particular career. All I can prove the existence of is the
fleeting subject of my present experiences, and this subject
may even be different in each moment. So the self may not be
a permanent and enduring thing, but just what is conscious
here and now.

Descartes could probably accept Russell's point at this stage
of his argument. He does, after all, say in *Meditation 2* '*I am,
I exist*, is necessarily true, every time I express it or conceive
of it in my mind' (p. 103) and '*I am, I exist*; this is certain;
but for how long? For as long as I think, for it might perhaps
happen, if I ceased to think, that I would at the same time
cease to be or to exist' (p. 105). Both remarks suggest that he

cannot be sure he exists as a permanent thing or person, and that he cannot *know* he exists except when actually performing the *cogito*.

Criticism 3 Hume is an empiricist and so believes that all our concepts must originate in experience, and more specifically in SENSATIONS or what Hume here calls PERCEPTIONS. Hume is asking us to perform an experiment: to look into our selves in search of our self. If we have a genuine concept of the self it must originate in some experience or perception. But, looking into himself, all he is aware of are perceptions of various sorts, none of which is a perception of himself. The self then is nothing over and above the perceptions we have. There is an awareness of perceptions but none of any owner of the perceptions. Hume concludes that the concept of 'self' merely refers to a bundle of perceptions without anything in which these perceptions occur.

If Hume is right, then this is a dangerous criticism for Descartes. For, as we shall see, he is going to want to argue that his self is indeed a thing, or substance, which has various conscious experiences and is not simply reducible to those experiences. So Descartes needs to take on Hume directly and insist, not implausibly, that for there to be conscious experiences it stands to reason that there must be a mind or thinker which is having those experiences. Thoughts cannot float free of thinkers; so if there are thoughts happening, which seems undeniable, there must be a self – the *I* – which is having them.

Criticism 4 Lichtenberg makes a similar point to Hume but approaches it from a different direction. He begins here by pointing out that language is important to the way we think. Language is itself a 'philosophy' in the sense that it shapes how we interpret and understand. For this reason, language can lead us astray and make us misinterpret things. An expression like 'I think' leads us to suppose that we are dealing with two things, as though the two words denoted distinct entities: the self and the thinking that it does. But this may be misleading. All that the immediate experience of consciousness allows us to conclude is that thinking is going on, or that 'it thinks', and not that there is a *self* or *I* doing the thinking. So, from the fact of doubting, Descartes cannot infer that there is something that doubts. Just because there is thinking it need not follow that there must be some *thing* or substance which thinks. After all if it is raining must there be some thing which rains?

As with Hume, Descartes' line of defence may be to insist that there must be a self for there to be thoughts. Here he may have to rely on a commitment to the general principle that for there to be any activity going on at all, there must be a substance to or in which it is taking place. Whether he should be allowed to appeal to such a principle at this stage, which he has not argued for after all, is a question we will return to.

Criticism 5 Wittgenstein is arguing that the self is not something which can enter into the world of experience. The self is like a window onto the world: it is a point of view from which we observe objects of experience, but not itself an object of experience. As we might put it: the self is only ever the *subject* of experience, never its *object*. To illustrate the idea he uses the analogy of an eye in its visual field. The eye cannot see itself; in other words, its visual field necessarily cannot encompass itself. And it is the same with consciousness. We are only ever conscious of experiences of various sorts, but cannot be conscious of the self which is conscious of these experiences.

This is another way of making a very similar point to that of Hume and Lichtenberg and so Descartes' response would need to be the same as to objections 3 and 4.

Criticism 6 Mersenne clearly believes that Descartes' discussion of what is established by the *cogito* in *Meditation 2* is supposed to establish the existence of his self as an immaterial substance which can exist independently of the brain. This interpretation is supported by the equivalent passage from the *Discourse* outlined at the beginning of the exercise, and by this remark from the *Meditations*: 'I am therefore, precisely speaking, only a thing which thinks, that is to say, a mind, understanding, or reason' (p. 105). But, Mersenne is saying, if we look into our mind or consciousness we may not be perceiving its true nature. I am conscious, yes, but what is consciousness exactly? What is the underlying mechanism which produces it? Of this I remain ignorant, so if Descartes is here trying to claim that I am in essence no more than consciousness, then his argument is premature. It could be that the mind is the product of some material processes going on in a physical brain, even though he hasn't yet established that such a thing exists.

As we shall see in *Meditation 6*, a central plank of Descartes' whole system is the claim that the self is indeed a non-physical or purely spiritual substance. Consciousness is not for him a product of the brain, and so we will be returning to Mersenne's critique in more detail when examining the later arguments for this position. However, here it is Mersenne who is being premature. At this stage Descartes is not claiming to have established that he is in essence a purely thinking substance. This is important as it is a common misinterpretation of Descartes' intentions at this stage. When Descartes says he is 'precisely speaking, only a thing which thinks' – despite appearances – he doesn't intend to say that he knows he is nothing more, as he explains in the discussion of this passage with Gassendi in the *Second Replies*.[21] All he intends to say is that all that he can, precisely speaking, establish at this stage is that he is a thinking thing. What exactly a thinking thing really is remains to be seen.

■ Further remarks on the *cogito*

▶ criticism ◀ Another significant point to consider is that, for the *cogito* to work, the Cartesian doubter must have at its disposal an array of fundamental concepts which it can manipulate clearly and rationally. Descartes must know what thought is, what doubt is, what existence is, and so forth, before he can put together the *cogito* argument; and yet the origin of these concepts is never questioned. So the doubts of the first *Meditation* do not, and nor are they intended to, undermine the very fabric of our conceptual apparatus. Descartes assumes that the content of our concepts, and the precise meaning of the terms he uses, are self evident; the only problem is to decide whether there exist things corresponding to them.[22] However, if he doesn't question the origin of these concepts then he runs the risk of not uncovering confusions or vagaries within them. Can he be sure he knows what the essential nature of thought or existence is? Could he be deceived into believing that he is thinking whereas something radically different is going on? We may recall here Lichtenberg's point that Descartes imports concepts uncritically into his analysis and so never questions what 'I' or 'thinking' are. If he did, he would have been able to focus on the experience itself and realise that there was no awareness of any distinction between thinking and the self. Such worries led some empiricist philosophers to complain that Descartes didn't pursue a radical enough project. Properly to start over from scratch would involve tracing the development of our very concepts from the first moment of consciousness.[23] Indeed, Descartes' approach can be seen as an effect of his rationalist prejudices with their tendency to regard many fundamental concepts as innate rather than derived from experience.

■ The importance of the *cogito*

As has been said, the *cogito* is one of the most discussed claims in the history of philosophy. But why has this short passage attracted so much attention?

One reason is the central importance of the *cogito* to Descartes' whole strategy. As a rationalist, Descartes intends to base his system of knowledge on truths discoverable by the use of reason alone, truths that can be understood simply by thinking about them without reference to sense experience. In his search for the building blocks of certainty, the *cogito* represents the first block. Because it is self-evident to any mind that cares to consider it, because it needs no further justification beyond itself, it provides Descartes with the ideal starting point from which to discover further such truths. Exactly how he uses the *cogito* to galvanise his rebuilding project will need to be examined below.

Secondly, and returning to a point made in the introduction, treating knowledge of his own mind as his starting point is emphatically to consider epistemology as first philosophy: it is to regard the manner in which we come to know the world as the foundation for further philosophical enquiries. As we saw in the introduction, this way of approaching metaphysical issues had a profound influence on the history of philosophy, even founding what is now called 'modern' philosophy.

The *cogito* has also attracted attention because of its apparent success in arresting the devastating sceptical advances of *Meditation 1*. Descartes here appears to have found a way to establish a piece of knowledge that is beyond even hyperbolic doubt and as such it represents a striking victory in the battle with scepticism. The *cogito* provides certain knowledge, not just about our ideas, but about at least one thing that exists in the world, namely myself. It is a substantive existential truth, not born out of experiment or observation, but of thought alone.

■ The Church and the *cogito*

For these reasons many thinkers since Descartes have followed him in treating the *cogito* as the proper starting place for philosophy. However, at the time, it landed Descartes in some trouble in certain theological circles. Some thought it improper, or even blasphemous, that Descartes should take his own existence to be the basis for a system of knowledge, rather than the existence of God. That Descartes' own mind should take centre stage and epistemic precedence was not thought to show the proper deference to the almighty.

Descartes' defence was to emphasise the distinction between two separate 'orders': the order of thought (*ordi cogniscendi*), by which we come to know things; and the order of existence (*ordi ordiniti*), by which things depend upon each other. In the order of thought, Descartes reckoned that he must claim knowledge of his own existence first. However, Descartes acknowledged that, in the order of existence, God comes first, of course, since he is the creator and sustainer of the universe.

Some initial observations on the nature of mind and body; sensation and imagination

Read *Meditation 2* paragraphs 5–9

The *cogito* may not look a very promising basis on which to reconstruct a body of knowledge. For it is not at all obvious that Descartes is going to be able to escape from the subjective realm of his own thinking and prove that anything beyond his consciousness exists. The Evil Demon Hypothesis is so radical that it appears impossible to dispel, and so all that Descartes would seem able to know about are his own mental states. If he is to remain true to his intention not to adopt any belief which is not indubitable, it looks as though he may be trapped in SOLIPSISM, that is to say, the belief that only me and the contents of my mind exist.

Nonetheless, in the remainder of the second *Meditation* Descartes begins the task of rebuilding his body of knowledge and does so by trying to show not only that knowledge of the *self* is clear, distinct and non-sensory, but also that we have a clear, distinct and non-sensory understanding of the appearance of MATERIAL *objects* or what he tends to call BODIES.

The nature of mind and of body

Who do you think you are?

1 Make a short list of the main attributes or characteristics that make you the person you are. These attributes may be physical characteristics, personality traits, habits or dispositions, etc.

2 Now subject each of these attributes to Cartesian doubt. In other words, try to imagine a scenario which would mean they weren't really part of you. Which of them are left over? Which are immune from doubt?

■ So what am I?

Although certain *that* he is, Descartes still doesn't know *what* he is (p. 103). In order to get clearer about what kind of thing he might be, he tries to strip away from his former opinion of what he is everything that is inessential to it, or everything that he cannot be certain is part of it. In this way he hopes the essential nature of his self will be left over – that which he can say indubitably that he is. So what did he formerly think he was? 'I thought I was a man. But what is a man' (pp. 103–4)? An initial definition he considers, one stemming from Aristotle, is that of a 'rational animal'.

However, he rejects the idea of starting from such an abstract definition since it would involve him in further questions concerning the meanings of the terms 'rational' and 'animal'. Instead he elects to pursue the more concrete idea he had of himself, one which he says sprang spontaneously from the consideration of his own nature, namely that of a physical body animated by a SOUL.

So, what exactly does the idea of a body entail? Descartes describes it as something which occupies a certain position in space, has a certain shape which is visible, tangible, etc. According to this notion of body, before its animation by the soul, it is not conscious, it cannot imagine or sense, have the power of self-movement or of nourishment. Thus the body itself is a 'machine made up of flesh and bones' akin to a 'corpse' (p. 104). So what of the soul? His idea of the soul was, Descartes tells us, of something like a subtle gas which is mixed throughout his body and which animates it, or brings it to life enabling it to nourish itself, to move about under its own power, to sense, imagine and think.

However, Descartes reasons, on the hypothesis of the all-powerful deceiver, he may not really have a 'face, hands, arms' or any of the 'machine made up of flesh and bones' (p. 104). For if his body is an illusion, any of the characteristics of himself as a body would not be a part of his nature (p. 105). And this means that his essential nature can be stripped of all those aspects which presuppose the existence of the body, meaning that he may not take up any space or have any shape.

But what of the soul which he had thought enabled him to eat, walk, feel and think? Well clearly, if he has no body, then he cannot eat or walk. Neither could he feel or sense anything since this would require having sense organs and objects to perceive. However, *thinking* or *consciousness* cannot be subtracted from his conception of his self. So thinking is certainly part of his nature since, as we have seen, it is required to perform the *cogito* and so cannot be doubted. So, while his body may not be part of him, thought definitely is. For as long as I am thinking, I must exist; and so, Descartes concludes, I must be a thinking thing, or conscious being; that is to say 'a MIND, understanding or reason' (p. 105).

Moreover, the definition of himself as a thinking thing does not depend on anything his senses seem to reveal about his having a body since he may not have one. As Descartes puts it: 'It is most certain … that this notion and knowledge of myself … do not depend on things the existence of which is not yet known to me' (p. 106). It is important to realise here that Descartes is not saying that his own existence as a thinking thing must be independent of the existence of his body, if he has one. This is a position he will only argue for in *Meditation 6*. For, as he says immediately before this remark, 'it may be that these same things that I suppose do not exist, because they are unknown to me, are not in truth different from me' (p. 106). Whether his body is distinct from him he says he cannot yet know and will not debate now. All he is saying is that his self-knowledge does not depend on his having knowledge of the existence of anything physical.

Sensation and imagination

Descartes wonders whether he might refine his understanding of his own nature by using his IMAGINATION. Now, 'imagining' in Descartes' terminology is 'nothing other than contemplating the figure or image of a corporeal object' (p. 106), in other words, it is the ability to conjure up images of physical things in our mind's eye, for example when dreaming. However, he reasons, since he is currently supposing that there are no physical things, the imagination, which like sensation (what Descartes calls 'perception', 'perceiving' or 'sensing') concerns physical bodies, cannot possibly give him a better understanding of himself.

However, Descartes continues to refine his conception of his self through the use of reason. I know I have the power to imagine and this is part of my thinking or consciousness; it is something of which I remain aware. And similarly sensation is something of which I am conscious. So these capacities are not distinct from thinking as such, or separate from what I am, because they are all acts of consciousness. So even if I am dreaming:

all the same, at least, it is very certain that it seems to me that I see light, hear a noise and feel a heat; and this is properly what in me is called perceiving and this, taken in this precise sense, is nothing other than thinking.
(p. 107, our emphasis)

Thus to the extent that sensation and imagination are treated as aspects of thought or consciousness – that is to say, simply in terms of the way these appear in the mind, and the extent to which they represent bodies is ignored – they can be considered part of my nature. This now provides a new and stricter definition of 'perceiving' or 'sensation' which no longer needs to make reference to the real existence of anything physical.

So Descartes has now established that he is a thinking thing, and by this he means a thing which 'doubts, perceives, affirms, denies, wills, does not will, that imagines also, and which feels' (p. 107). What this means is that his conscious life, which is to say his self or mind, consists of these different aspects or 'faculties'. So in summary we can say that the mind has the following faculties:

- INTELLECT or UNDERSTANDING, i.e. the faculty which engages in rational thought, such as when doing philosophy or mathematics.
- WILL, i.e. the faculty which makes me free to think what I choose, say when I decide to think about Descartes' arguments or follow any train of thought whatever.
- Imagination, i.e. the faculty which enables us to conjure the images of physical things before our mind's eye, as when for example one imagines a unicorn, or a sexual fantasy.
- Sensation, i.e. the faculty which perceives the images of physical things, as when I see a table before me. It is important to stress that, 'sensation' here does not necessarily involve the actual existence of the object perceived, but merely the way it appears in my mind.

So Descartes thinks he is a thinking *thing*. In other words, his claim is that he is a substance with certain *attributes* or MODES. These modes are different types of conscious state, such as willing, denying, sensing and imagining. And all these different modes are modes of one and the same self.

■ Figure 5.2
Descartes is a thinking thing

Descartes' mind has various modes. These he is directly conscious of. The world beyond the mind is still not known to exist. But even if the physical world doesn't exist, Descartes can still know that sensations appear in his mind.

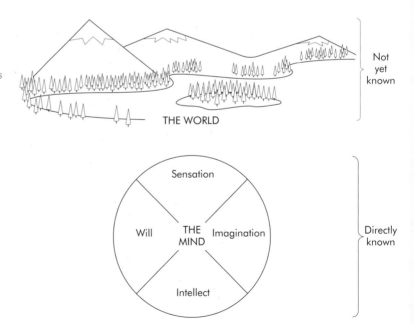

THE WORLD

Not yet known

Sensation

Will　　THE MIND　Imagination

Intellect

Directly known

Interpretation and evaluation

Up to this point, the modern reader has not struggled to understand the conceptual language that Descartes has been employing. The concepts of doubt, certainty, thought and existence have not changed radically in the last few centuries. However, as Descartes starts to examine the nature of the self he begins to use a variety of technical concepts from the philosophy of his day which are not now part of ordinary discourse. The first of these is the distinction between *substances* and *modes*.

Substances and modes

The theoretical distinction between *substances* and *modes* is between those things that can exist on their own and don't depend on anything else for their existence (substances), and those that cannot exist on their own and depend on substances for their existence (modes). This distinction is perhaps clearest if we consider an example of a physical object such as a knob of butter. The butter itself is a substance or piece of stuff. It can exist in its own right. But its colour cannot. The colour has to be the colour *of* something. So the colour is a *mode* of the butter and depends on the butter for its existence. A mode, then, is a property or an attribute of a substance and it needs the substance to exist. In a similar way, Descartes is arguing in these passages, my self or mind is a substance, and the different types of conscious experience I enjoy are different modes I can undergo. So understanding, willing, imagining and sensing are all modes of consciousness.

This effectively means that sensations can be viewed purely as a type of thought or consciousness; in other words as a certain category of conscious experience. And, importantly, this means that the fact that we experience sensation does not commit us to any beliefs about the material things and processes which we may normally associate with it, i.e. the sense organs and the effects made on them by physical objects. So sensations can be attributed to me as a conscious being regardless of whether or not my body or other bodies really exist.

An equivalent point is being made concerning 'imagination', or the faculty which conjures images of material things before the mind's eye. For similarly an act of imagination can be viewed simply as an act of consciousness and it exists as such regardless of whether the imagined objects are real. So the mind – as defined at this stage – is a substance whose modes include understanding, willing, as well as sensing and imagining.

Particular acts of the understanding, the will, imagination or sensation are called ACCIDENTS. So if I am working out a sum, willing my arm to move, imagining a wintry scene, or smelling a ripe mango, these are particular *accidents* of these modes of thought.

■ The thinker and the thinking

▶ criticism ◀

So for Descartes to call himself a thinking *thing* is to say that he is a substance which has thoughts and other conscious experiences, and so he has distinguished the thinker from the thoughts it thinks. Now, as you will have seen when going through the *cogito* exercise, an important objection to Descartes' use of the *cogito* is that he thinks it self-evident that if there is consciousness or thought there must be a thinker. But we can argue that all that is actually established in the *cogito* is that there are thoughts or conscious experiences going on. Nothing in the experience of these experiences allows us to conclude that there is a thinker – I – which is having these thoughts. Descartes is assuming that conscious experiences are modes of a substance, but they could be substances in their own right existing independently. Even if we reject the idea that we could have free-floating experiences without a mind in or to which they occur, we can at least object that to know this Descartes must make implicit reference to a theory that everything is either a substance or a mode. And whether or not this is right, if Descartes is making implicit use of it in the *cogito*, we might complain that he is incorporating a general principle uncritically and violating the basic principles of his method of doubt.

■ The essence of the self

In trying to find the nature of the 'I' Descartes is employing the idea of an essential feature or property (although he does not actually use the term ESSENCE in the Penguin translation). By stripping away what is inessential his intention is to discover what is essential to his self or mind. But what exactly is an essence? Below are two possible uses of the concept of essence:

1 Approaching the issue from an *objective* point of view, the essence of something is that without which a thing would not be that thing.
2 Approaching the issue from a *subjective* point of view – i.e. from the perspective of a human mind considering something – an essence is that without which you cannot conceive that thing as being that thing.

For example, think of a large red triangle. Would it still be a triangle if it were blue or yellow? Clearly it would. Would it still be a triangle if it were a bit bigger or smaller? Again the obvious answer is 'Yes'. What this shows is that size and colour are not part of the essence of a triangle since changing these features does not prevent it from still being a triangle. These are termed its 'accidental' features. But would it still be a triangle if it had more or fewer sides? Clearly not, for having three sides is an essential feature of a triangle – a feature it cannot do without – as it would not be a triangle with as few as two, or with as many as four sides. Also, subjectively, it is impossible to conceive of a triangle with two sides or four, so on this second definition it is also an essential feature. Here the subjective and objective ways of searching for the essence have the same answer: a triangle must have three sides.

experimenting with ideas

In the first two columns below are listed the essences of various things alongside specific examples of such things. In the other three columns are certain properties possessed by these things. Which of these propertiess could safely be removed without changing the essential nature of the thing, i.e. without its becoming something else?

Essences of things	Particular examples of such things	1 If we take away this property does it still have the same essence?	2 If we take away this property does it still have the same essence?	3 If we take away this property does it still have the same essence?
Triangle	Large red triangle	Its large size	Its red colour	Its three sides
Chair	Comfortable arm chair	Its comfortable cushions	Having two arms	All its legs
Boat	Sea-worthy sailing boat	The sail	Being made of wood	Its capacity to float on water
Tree	Blossoming cherry tree	Its blossom	Its leaves	Its trunk
Statue	Wax statue of Descartes	Its large size	Its yellowy colour	Its shape (we melt it)
Wax	Wax statue of Descartes	Its yellow colour	Its shape (we melt it)	Its solidity (we evaporate it)
Self or I	Descartes	His name	His memories	His body

Descartes in the passage overleaf is exploring the nature of the 'I' that thinks. He concludes that there are many things that he is not.

I am not this assemblage of limbs called the human body: I am not a thin and penetrating air spread through all these members; I am not a wind, a breath of air, a vapour, or anything else that I can invent or imagine, … and yet … I find that I am nevertheless certain that I am something. (pp. 105–106)

His claim is that he can conceive of himself existing – being *something* – without conceiving of all these other things: a body, a vapour, etc. So here he is using the subjective approach in determining his essence. These things cannot be part of his essential nature, as, from the subjective point of view, an essence is that without which you cannot conceive a thing as being that thing – and he clearly can conceive of himself without a body etc. So if he is *not* these things what then *is* he?

Another attribute is thinking, and I here discover an attribute which does belong to me; this alone cannot be detached from me. (p. 105)

Here Descartes suggests that he cannot detach the idea of thinking from that of himself. In other words, he can't conceive of himself not thinking. So again, according to the subjective approach, thinking appears to be an essential attribute of his mind.

▶ criticism ◀ Although this line of thinking may seem straightforward it raises several philosophical problems. Firstly, it is important to note that what might count as an essential feature of an object depends on how that object is described. For example, consider a wax statue of Descartes. Would it still be a *statue of Descartes* if it were placed too closely to the fire and melted into a waxy blob? No, it wouldn't. When described as a *statue of Descartes*, the shape becomes an essential feature – lose the shape and you lose the statue of Descartes. However, would it still be a *lump of wax* if it were placed next to the fire and melted? Yes it would. Described as a *lump of wax* the shape is not an essential feature. Would it still be a *lump of wax* if it were sent to a chemical processing plant and turned into paraffin, then into a thousand plastic bags? Probably not. The chemical composition would have changed and most people would view this as an essential feature of anything counting as a *lump of wax*.

What this suggests is that before Descartes conducts a search into the essence of his self he needs to define it. But different definitions will produce different results. If he is being defined as a philosopher, or a human being, then it might well seem that a body *would* be an essential feature. However, Descartes seems to be searching for the essence of 'I' without having any definition of what this might be.

▶ criticism ◀ Secondly, Descartes is using the subjective approach in establishing his essential nature. He has to do this because he has no objective understanding of what his self is. All he can know is the way he appears to himself, because his whole approach involves relying on how things appear to his mind. But this leads to problems, for in order to discover the essential nature of something we surely need to have an objective understanding of what it is. To see this, consider how scientists would approach the task of uncovering the essence of something, say water. What they certainly would not do is approach it using the subjective approach: they would not sit around and work out what properties they could and couldn't conceive water as having. At most, this would tell them a bit about the human concept of water (what is sometimes termed the 'nominal essence'). It might also tell them something about what they can and cannot conceive as humans, in other words about their own intellectual limitations. But such an approach would not win a Nobel prize. To determine the essential nature of water a scientist is going to need to conduct experiments and tests which might reveal its chemical composition and this can be done only by engaging with the stuff itself, not just one's thoughts about it. So trying to unearth the essence of an object based on what you can and cannot conceive is not a method modern science would accept as sound. Such an approach is likely to lead to fallacious thinking. The exact nature of the FALLACY in question will be examined later (see the section on the masked-man fallacy – page 133), but the heart of the difficulty is that Descartes' ability to *conceive* himself without a body does not imply that his own essence must be immaterial.

However, these criticisms do depend on our viewing Descartes as attempting a definitive answer to the question of what he is at this stage of his enquiry. He says that these observations make him a little better acquainted with himself (p. 107), but the idea that he thinks he has established his *essential* nature is premature for the reasons we have discussed. Descartes has been exploring the way he appears to himself and has established that thought is one quality that cannot be separated from himself, but (as the *Replies* make clear) he cannot yet claim that his self is essentially thought: that he is nothing more than a thinking thing. Although certain remarks do seem to suggest this stronger claim, he does not directly argue this until the sixth *Meditation* when he completes his account of the distinction between mind and body.

So, in terms of the overall structure of the *Meditations*, Descartes would be unable to prove such claims about the mind and body at this stage since they would not be demon-proof, i.e. they are not self-evident or self-verifying like the *cogito* itself. He has only just established that he exists – and only then because the thought is self-verifying. So we need to read these exploratory remarks about himself as laying the ground for the later arguments. Here Descartes is just exploring the way he appears to himself, but not making any firm claims about his true nature from an objective perspective. So while he can conclude the section by saying that 'I begin to know what I am, a little more clearly and distinctly than hitherto', he falls short of saying that he knows what he is for certain.

Key points: Chapter 5

What you need to know about *Meditation 2* – the *cogito* and the nature of the mind:

1 Descartes attempts to push his doubts even further. If the world may not exist, might it not also be that he doesn't exist either? However, the attempt to doubt his own existence reveals that he must exist. He cannot doubt his own existence as to do so he must be thinking and if he is thinking, he must exist. So, if he is deceived at all, he must be something.

2 But what is he? Since he is conscious he must be a thinking thing or conscious being. And all 'modes' of his consciousness must be part of what he is.

3 Looking into his mind Descartes enumerates the different 'modes' of his consciousness that he discovers. Firstly he has an understanding or intellect, i.e. that in him which enables him to reason. He has a will which enables him to make choices and decide what to think or believe. He has an imagination which is his ability to picture physical things. And finally he has sensations, i.e. an awareness of experiences which appear to come from his body and through his sense organs.

4 Importantly, Descartes observes that sensation, considered purely as a mode of his consciousness, is something he is directly aware of and can know he experiences, even while he is as yet unsure that any physical things exist beyond his mind, including his own body.

6
Meditation 2: The experiment with the wax

Knowledge of the wax

Read *Meditation 2*
paragraphs 10–18

Descartes elects to turn his attention from the nature of mind to that of matter (p. 108ff.). For he observes that, despite what has been said, he cannot help thinking that he knows material bodies more distinctly than he does himself. It is important to recognise that the ensuing discussion is an analysis of matter *as it appears to his mind*. In other words it stays true to the Evil Demon Hypothesis by continuing to suspend judgement about the independent existence of material bodies. He argues as follows.

Do our senses perceive the wax?

A body, such as a piece of wax (which Descartes will use as an example of material bodies as such), has specific perceivable properties that appear to our senses (a certain taste, smell, colour, temperature, texture, hardness, shape, size, etc.) by which we recognise it and normally suppose we have a distinct idea of it and what it is like. However, if the wax is heated these properties change. It changes colour, temperature, size, shape, its smell, etc. Indeed, in the case of a piece of wax, when heated, *all* its original properties change. So is it then the same wax? Certainly our normal judgement is that it is. Assuming it is, Descartes asks 'what, then, was it that I knew in this piece of wax with such distinctness?' (p. 108). In other words, how did I judge it to be the same? Clearly it cannot be because of any of the perceived properties which have changed, and so this judgement cannot be based on what our senses tell us. For nothing I can taste, smell, see, touch or hear is the same. So what we think of as remaining is not the properties perceived by the senses, but rather the substance of the wax: the stuff underlying these perceptual qualities.

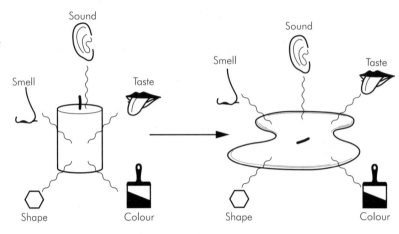

■ Figure 6.1

All the properties our senses perceive in the wax change when it is melted. So nothing that we can see, smell, feel, hear or taste is the same form when it is solid as when it is liquid. So it cannot be our senses which make us suppose it is the same.

Does the imagination perceive the wax?

So what is our idea of substance or of material *body*? And how do we apprehend it if not by the senses? Descartes' answer to the first question is that our idea of body is of something 'extended, flexible and malleable' (p. 109). In other words it is of something that takes up space or which is three-dimensional, and which can change its shape within those three dimensions. So what of the second question: could it be by the *imagination* that we perceive this body? As we have seen, the imagination, for Descartes, is our capacity to conjure the images of material things before our mind's eye. But we cannot imagine or visualise all the possible states the wax is capable of being in while remaining the same piece of wax, and therefore it cannot be our imagination which regards it as the same. So, Descartes concludes, we do not apprehend the piece of wax with our imagination.

Does the understanding perceive the wax?

So if it is not by sensation and not by imagination that we apprehend the wax, what is it? Descartes thinks the only option left is the intellect or understanding. Only the intellect can recognise the wax to be capable of infinite changes. What I recognise to remain through all the changes, namely the *body* or substance of the wax, must therefore be *judged* to be there. In other words it is apprehended by a purely *mental* perception or what Descartes calls an 'intuition of the mind' (p. 110). This intuition is, he tells us, clear and distinct. And what is judged to remain through all the infinite possible changes is simply something which occupies some space or, as Descartes has it, is 'extended'. In other words, we judge the essential nature of the wax lying beneath its outer appearance to be three-dimensionality or EXTENSION. Recall that

Descartes is not yet making any claims about the existence of the wax or any material things. Rather he is trying to determine its essential nature by stripping down his idea of it to its essentials. The question of whether there is anything corresponding to his idea of the wax as pure extension will have to wait until *Meditation 6* for an answer.

Looking at people in the street

Descartes likens the situation to looking out of the window onto people on the street below. Normally we are inclined to say that we can 'see' the people. However, if they are heavily dressed, strictly speaking we may only be seeing their hats and coats, in other words, their outer clothing. So we don't really *see* people at all, but rather *judge* that they are there beneath the clothes. In a sense, then, it is our *mind* which perceives the people, not our eyes. In the same way, Descartes claims, it is not our eyes or our other senses which perceive the wax. Rather it is our mind which penetrates through the outer appearance seen by the senses and with a kind of intellectual vision, or 'an intuition of the mind', perceives the essential nature of the wax.

To perceive the wax in this way, Descartes claims, requires a human mind, and so he can complete his discussion of the wax by claiming that the experiment has made his knowledge of himself a little clearer. He must have a mind in order to perceive the wax at all. And so his own existence as a thinking mind is now more certain still than that of the wax. For, whether or not the wax actually exists, the fact that I can judge that it does, means that I must exist.

■ **Figure 6.2**

The senses only perceive the outer appearance of the wax. The mind, however, perceives its essential nature by a clear and distinct 'intuition'. In other words, recognising that the wax remains despite the changes it has undergone must involve more than the senses: it requires a judgement of our understanding. The essential nature judged to remain in the wax is something extended in three-dimensional space.

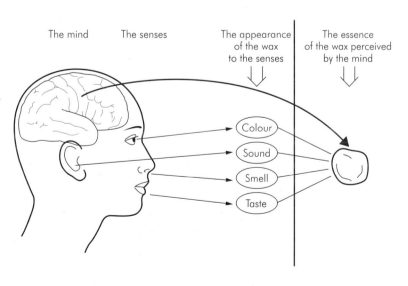

The mind   The senses   The appearance of the wax to the senses   The essence of the wax perceived by the mind

Colour

Sound

Smell

Taste

Interpretation and evaluation

■ The wax is a substance with modes and an essential nature

Just as Descartes earlier claimed that his self was a substance and that it had various attributes or modes, so here he now draws the same distinction with respect to the wax. The wax is also conceived by the mind to be substance with various modes.

Descartes also identifies what he considers to be the essential nature of the wax:

Let us consider it attentively, and setting aside everything that does not belong to the wax, let us see what remains. Indeed nothing remains except something extended, flexible and malleable. (p. 109)

'Extended, flexible and malleable' are the only qualities that Descartes cannot conceive of the wax without. These, he is saying, are essential to his idea of the wax. So if physical things do exist, then their essence will include these features. Extension in three dimensions, in other words, is an essential mode that any physical object must have. It is inconceivable that an object exist without these qualities.

► criticism ◄

However, again we may call into question this subjective approach to the discovery of the essence of something. Compare this with the methods a modern scientist might employ to try to establish the essential nature of the wax, namely practical experimentation. Simply contemplating the wax as it appears to the mind is not going to give us any very interesting objective knowledge of what it is really made of; at best it will be an interesting analysis of its appearance to a human mind.

Again, though, we need to be careful before pressing home this objection at this stage. For here Descartes is not yet attempting to discover the objective essence of the wax, he is merely laying the ground for his later arguments which will claim that the essence of matter is extension in space. For now, he is aware that all he can do is analyse the way a physical thing like the wax appears in his mind, since he as yet has no knowledge of whether it even exists. However, Descartes was one of the modern scientists of his day and his treatment of the wax does show how different his approach was from that of the scientists that went before. A scholastic thinker would probably infuse a lump of wax with a multitude of properties, perhaps waxiness, flammability and morphability, to name a few. Descartes, although only speculating at this point, is keen to suggest what he believes to be its real properties. Unlike the scholastic, these are reduced to a few, and these few qualities are ones that can be measured and recorded and studied. Although outmoded now, Descartes' way of approaching the nature of the wax was part of the scientific revolution sweeping the seventeenth century.

■ Is Descartes drawing the primary/secondary quality distinction?

Since the conclusion that the sensed properties were not *distinctly* comprehended in the wax is supposed to follow from the observation that the sensed properties change without the wax ceasing to be, it would seem that Descartes wants to argue that distinct comprehension has to do with grasping the unchanging or permanent properties of a thing. This suggests that Descartes may be drawing a distinction here not unlike that between what are termed the PRIMARY and SECONDARY QUALITIES of objects; in other words between those qualities an object has independently of any perceiving mind, such as size and shape, and those qualities which appear to be in objects, such as colours and smells, but which are really powers that these objects have to produce such sensations in us. According to this distinction, the colour of an object, for example, is not really in the object itself, in the way its shape is. Rather, the colour sensation is produced in our minds by the way in which the object interacts with our sense organs; perhaps by the way its molecular structure reflects the light rays picked up by our eyes.

With this in mind it is plausible to suppose that in this passage Descartes is saying that because I can conceive of an object without any colour, smell, etc. but cannot conceive of an object without any size and position, this shows that size and position are essential to my idea of body. So those properties of physical objects which can be described geometrically and mathematically, principally their extension and mobility, and which are perceived 'clearly and distinctly', are the essential properties of these objects: those they must have if they exist. And those properties such as colour and odour, which cannot be understood in geometric or mathematical terms, and which are not understood 'clearly and distinctly', are not essential and so would not be real properties of objects, if they exist. This interpretation of Descartes' intentions here would fit well, as we shall see, with his considered view of the essential nature of body which is discussed below when we get on to *Meditation 6*. There he argues that extension is essential to material bodies, but all other perceived properties are explained in terms of how these objects affect our minds. Colours, sounds and smells are not really out there, whereas size, position and shape are.

▶ criticism ◀ However, one obvious problem with this interpretation is Descartes' focus on the idea that he can subtract the wax's properties of colour, smell, etc. in a way he cannot with its properties of being 'extended, flexible and malleable'. For, while the odour and colour *change*, the wax retains *some* colour and smell throughout. In fact neither set of properties is unchanging. Its shape changes just as much as does its colour. And while it always retains *some* shape, no less must it retain *some* colour. Although it remains extended and flexible, it also remains coloured and smelly. For this reason, it doesn't seem as though Descartes' experiment draws the distinction between primary and secondary properties in the way he might hope.

■ The mind or understanding *judges* the wax to be there

Despite this difficulty, it is clear that the conclusion that the wax has been understood all along by the mind alone rather than by imagination or sensation relies on the observation that I recognise the wax to be the same regardless of its various transformations. The wax appears to be more than the set of perceivable or imaginable properties. Here the idea seems to be that, since nothing that has been observed by the senses has remained constant, the recognition that the wax is the same must be made by the mind. Since imagination is restricted to what it actually observes and cannot imagine innumerable variations, the *judgement* that it is the same wax must be the work of the understanding.

Descartes is arguing that I do not see the *wax* as such but merely its sensed qualities, just as I do not see people in the street, but merely their clothing (p. 110). And yet I think of it as more than the finite set of qualities I have seen or can imagine. So I do not know the wax simply in virtue of seeing it. By 'unclothing' the wax of its inessential sensed appearance, the human mind is left to contemplate its true nature. In other words, I can subtract its outer appearance from my idea of the wax, leaving a pure idea of an extended thing. It is this, claims Descartes, that I clearly and distinctly understand. So while before it seemed that I knew the wax *distinctly* in virtue of its falling beneath my senses, it now appears that I know it precisely to the extent that I withdraw from the senses. Note again that on this interpretation Descartes is not yet claiming to know what the essential properties of body are, but simply that it is most clearly and distinctly known by thought, not sense or imagination.

■ Why does Descartes know himself better now?

Finally, what does Descartes' claim to have shown that the mind is now 'better' known than the body amount to? Part of his idea is that I can know myself more clearly than I can know any body that appears to the senses, since a condition of possibility for my judging (rightly or wrongly) that any other thing exists is my own existence. In other words, I have first to exist in order to perceive the wax. However, why this should amount to knowing the mind 'better' is not so obvious. Gassendi, for example, remarks in the fifth *Objections* that to know something of the true nature of a substance is to have an understanding of its internal constitution. And while Descartes may have shown that the mind *exists*, he has failed to reveal anything much about it.

It may be that all Descartes has in mind by saying that he knows himself better is simply that he knows himself more certainly. For the existence of himself is given implicitly in the very act of perception, while the existence of the objects perceived remains doubtful. His idea may be that every conscious act involves a kind of implicit awareness of the existence of the self which is conscious.

Alternatively, the claim to know himself better may mean that he understands his capacities better, in the sense that he now knows that it is his understanding, rather than his senses or imagination, which is most centrally involved in the perception of physical things, whether or not they actually exist.

A related point may be that he now realises that knowledge of bodies will always be indirect, and so subject to doubt, whereas his *self*-knowledge is not like this. Knowledge of his own mind is direct, and so he can now make progress by focusing on his own mind and seeing what he can usefully find there which might form the basis for making progress in his quest for knowledge.

■ We don't perceive bodies by the understanding alone

▶ criticism ◀ Whatever Descartes precisely intends, we can certainly resist his more forceful claim, namely that what perceives the wax is 'only an intuition of the mind' (p. 110). For it is surely absurd to say that we can know about physical things around us completely independently of the senses. After all, we wouldn't even suppose them to be there if we had no sense experiences. So while we may accept that the mind is necessary for perceiving the wax in the way we do, it is surely not sufficient.

Descartes' rationalism inclines him to emphasise the superiority of the understanding over the senses, and this remark should be understood in this context. Descartes thought that science and philosophy could be conducted largely by the use of reason; and the wax passage is primarily concerned to undermine the common-sense and empiricist view that we can come to know physical things simply by the avenue of our senses. So reason will be the key by which to unlock an understanding of the essence of matter and which will establish the framework for scientific understanding of the material world. However, any suggestion that reason *alone* could discover the details of what exists and how nature actually works would be overstating Descartes' case, for he is aware that sensation will have a role to play in determining the details within the framework discovered by reason.

Key points: Chapter 6

What you need to know about *Meditation 2* – the experiment with the wax:

1 Descartes turns his attention to the way material things appear to his mind, and elects to contemplate his perception of a piece of wax as an example.

2 He observes that the wax appears to have a series of perceptible qualities, such as colour, smell, size, shape and so on. These are what he had believed allowed him to perceive the wax.

3 However, he notices that when the wax is heated all these perceived qualities change. The wax becomes a different colour, acquires a different smell, expands, changes shape and so on. So none of the original qualities by which he appeared to perceive the wax is any longer present.

4 And this presents Descartes with a problem, for ordinarily he still regards it as the same piece of wax, yet nothing he perceives by his senses is the same. This shows, he concludes, that the senses cannot after all be what perceives the wax.

5 So could it be by his imagination that he perceives the wax? Descartes dismisses this possibility on the grounds that his idea of the wax includes the understanding that the changes it could undergo are infinite, and yet he is unable to *imagine* all these possible changes.

6 Of his faculties, this leaves only his intellect or understanding as what perceives the wax. Descartes claims that his intellect recognises the essence of the wax by 'intuition', or a purely mental inspection. The mind judges it to be in essence something extended in space.

7 Descartes draws an analogy of his perception of the wax with his perception of people in the street wearing hats and coats. In the latter case he does not actually see the people themselves. Rather his mind is involved in judging that there are people underneath the coats and hats that he does see. In the same way, when perceiving the wax, his senses perceive only the outer appearance, while the mind judges that the substance or essence of the wax persists beneath this appearance.

8 Descartes concludes the *Meditation* by saying that he now knows himself better, for while the existence of the wax remains in doubt, his own existence is certain, since he must exist to have any perception of the wax.

7

Meditations 3 and 4: The Trademark Argument; error and the will

Clear and distinct ideas

Read *Meditation 3* paragraphs 1 and 2

In the first few paragraphs of *Meditation 3*, Descartes recaps on what has been established over the first two *Meditations*. He now knows that his nature as a thinking thing is for him to doubt, assert, deny, understand, but also to imagine and sense: so it involves understanding, will, imagination and sensation. Of these 'modes of thought' he can be certain, even while he remains uncertain of the existence of his own and other physical bodies. So what he knows is that he is a conscious being or thinking thing.

Now Descartes asks himself what is distinctive about the knowledge so far acquired. In other words, what is it that makes it certain? If he can find some distinguishing feature of this knowledge it may help him to discover some further pieces of knowledge; it may, in other words, provide him with a way to identify other TRUTHS. Descartes' answer is that what makes the *cogito* certain is that he has a *clear and distinct* understanding of it. This observation leads him to suppose that whatever else he understands clearly and distinctly may also be true: '… it seems to me that I can already establish as a general rule that all the things we conceive very clearly and distinctly are true' (p. 113). So this will be the mark or criterion by which Descartes can identify true beliefs.

Interpretation and evaluation

■ What does Descartes mean by 'clear and distinct ideas'?

Descartes' notion of 'clear and distinct ideas' plays a crucial role in the development of his theory of knowledge. Since he reckons that anything clearly and distinctly perceived will be true, he will attempt to rebuild his body of knowledge using such ideas as his foundations. So it is important for us to determine what he means by these terms.

From his other writings it is apparent that clear and distinct ideas will be those which can be grasped by what Descartes calls INTUITION, in other words understood by his intellect or understanding by the LIGHT OF REASON. He writes:

> *By intuition I do not mean the fluctuating testimony of the senses, or the deceptive judgement of the imagination as it botches things together, but the conception of a clear and attentive mind, which is so easy and distinct that there can be no room for doubt about what we are understanding. Alternatively, and this comes to the same thing, intuition is the indubitable conception of a clear and attentive mind which proceeds solely from the light of reason ... Thus everyone can mentally intuit that he exists, that he is thinking, that a triangle is bounded by just three sides, and a sphere by a single surface, and the like.*[24]

This suggests that 'intuited' truths are truths of reason, or truths recognisable *a priori*. So clear and distinct ideas are beliefs we can acquire just by thinking about them within the understanding, without reference to imagination or sensation. And it is these clear and distinct ideas upon which Descartes' foundationalism will rest. They are the self-justifying and self-evident beliefs upon which he hopes to build 'something firm and constant in the sciences' (p. 98).

Recall also that, alongside the *cogito* and simple geometric truths, Descartes also claims we have a clear and distinct understanding of the essence of our idea of matter, as was shown in the wax experiment of *Meditation 2*. There we were told that his idea of the wax is of something extended in space, and this is perceived by a 'clear and distinct' 'intuition of the mind' (p. 110). By this he appears to mean that there is nothing obscure in his idea of material substance, although, we must recall, he is not making claims about its independent existence.

■ Can knowledge be defined in terms of being clear and distinct?

▶ criticism ◀ As we have seen, Descartes puts the success of the *cogito* down to the fact that its truth can be grasped clearly and distinctly. He then generalises this principle and claims that any belief he can conceive clearly and distinctly must also be true, and so he can claim certain knowledge of such beliefs. But is this a valid generalisation to make? One concern we may have is that it is based on very thin evidence. Although *one* belief may be knowable because it can be grasped clearly and distinctly, this can hardly be a sound basis to conclude that *any* belief grasped in this way must also be true. After all, wouldn't this be a bit like observing one pink pig and then concluding that all pigs must be pink? Any generalisation of this sort is not guaranteed to throw up true conclusions; after all, pigs are not always pink. So how can Descartes claim that all beliefs grasped in this way are guaranteed to be true?

▶ criticism ◀ There is another key reason to doubt his use of the clear and distinct criterion, and this doubt is based on an analysis of the concept of truth. 'Truth' is a word that applies to judgements and beliefs, and not to objects. Sentences such as 'There are five cows in the field' or 'Michelle is pregnant' can be true or false because they express a judgement about the world; whereas it makes no sense to point at an object, say a rock, or a banana, and call it true or false. So the term 'truth' applies to sentences, utterances, written statements and beliefs – anything with 'propositional content': anything, in other words, which asserts something to be the case. But what has to happen for a belief to be true?

There are different, competing theories as to the nature of truth. One of the most popular and intuitively plausible says that it consists in a correspondence between the belief and the relevant fact. According to this, the *correspondence* theory, a belief is true just if what it claims is the case actually is the case. And if there is no fact corresponding with what the belief says then it is false.

■ **Figure 7.1 The correspondence theory of truth**
Here the belief corresponds exactly to the fact, so the belief is true. If there were one or three or no pigs, then the belief would not correspond to the fact and so would be false. According to this theory, truth consists in this correspondence between belief and fact.

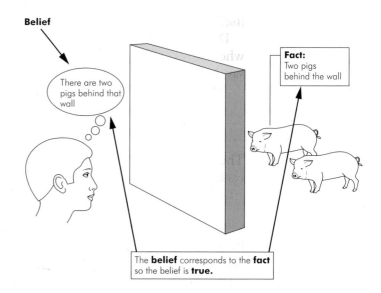

Belief

There are two pigs behind that wall

Fact:
Two pigs behind the wall

The **belief** corresponds to the **fact** so the belief is **true.**

However, Descartes, in suggesting that any clearly and distinctly apprehended belief must be true, is doing away with the idea of any correspondence criteria. He is suggesting that just by examining the belief alone we can tell if a judgement is true or not. If the idea is clear and distinct enough, it is true. Under this system there is no need to check the judgement against any corresponding fact.

The philosopher Gilbert Ryle has strongly criticised this position. Ryle compares the concept of truth with the act of scoring of a goal in football:

To score a goal you need:
a) to kick/head the ball,
b) for the ball to end up in the net.

And in the same way:

For a belief to be true you need:
a) a belief,
b) the belief to correspond to the fact.

Descartes believes that we can establish the truth just by examining a), the nature of the belief, and by seeing how clear and distinct it is. Ryle suggests that this is like trying to tell whether you have scored a goal just by focusing on the shot. But this plainly does not work. You may have struck the ball beautifully, but this does not necessarily mean it will end up in the goal. You cannot tell you have scored by focusing on the strike of the ball alone. Likewise you cannot tell whether a belief is true just by focusing on the belief itself.

Descartes is using only 'internal' criteria to establish whether a belief is true and can count as knowledge, that is to say, he looks exclusively within the belief itself. However, in doing so, Descartes is going against most theories of truth which, like the correspondence theory, require an 'external' criterion.

The case of the *cogito*, however, would seem to be an exception to this criticism. It seems we can know the *cogito* is true just by examining the belief itself. This might be because the belief 'I am, I exist' is confirmed in the very act of asserting it. The same utterance simultaneously acts as the belief and proves the relevant fact which is being claimed. So, in the case of the *cogito*, the belief and the fact coincide, which is why we called it 'self-verifying'. But even if we accept this for the *cogito* this is emphatically *not* the case for most other beliefs. The *cogito* is a very special kind of belief: one for which thinking it makes it true, but this character cannot be generalised to other beliefs. So at best Descartes might be able to say that all self-justifying beliefs must be true, but not that all beliefs recognisable clearly and distinctly must be.

■ How can we be sure which beliefs really are clear and distinct?

▶ criticism ◀ Even if we accept that recognising a belief clearly and distinctly is enough to guarantee its truth, there are still problems. For how precisely can Descartes be sure that he really does clearly and distinctly understand a belief? Isn't it possible that he *seems* to understand something clearly and distinctly, but does not in fact do so? After all, it is quite possible to make mistakes, even in simple judgements, as Descartes himself points out in *Meditation 1*. So could I not be mistaken into thinking a belief is clear and distinct when it is not? Couldn't the demon fool me into thinking I can clearly and distinctly recognise that 2 + 3 make 5 when I can't?

To avoid making such a mistake, Descartes would appear to need some criteria to apply by which to distinguish those beliefs which he understands clearly and distinctly from those he does not. But if he could find such criteria, the same problem would loom again: how can he be sure he is applying *these* criteria correctly? Again the difficulty is that it is always possible that what seems to be making the distinction properly may not in fact be. To answer that he can clearly and distinctly perceive that he is applying them correctly obviously will not do, as this simply invites the question of how he can be *sure* of this, and so a vicious infinite regress looms.

Descartes needs to prove God exists to dispel his radical doubts

Read *Meditation 3* paragraphs 3–5

We have seen that Descartes hopes he can use the clear and distinct criterion in order to identify beliefs which are guaranteed to be knowledge. However, before he is prepared to move forward on this assumption he thinks he needs first to dispel any remaining doubts concerning clear and distinct beliefs. Can they really be relied upon? After all, as he reminds us, he used to think that he clearly and distinctly perceived that physical objects existed outside of his perception of them and that they resembled his perception of them. But while he may have been correct in this assumption, he certainly didn't know it by the light of reason (p. 114). So it is possible to think you perceive something clearly and distinctly when you don't. Moreover, he has argued in *Meditation 1* that, even when it comes to simple mathematical judgements, or to counting the sides of a square, it is conceivable that he can go wrong – if, that is, there is a powerful deceiving God or demon. So it is *possible* that even beliefs perceived clearly and distinctly are false. Now while this reason for doubt about his reasoning faculties 'is very slight, and, so to speak, metaphysical' (p. 115), it is nonetheless necessary to establish some sort of guarantee that what is perceived clearly and distinctly really is true and reliable. Only in this way can his further epistemological progress be immunised from error. So:

> *in order to be able to remove this doubt completely, I must inquire whether there is a God, as soon as the opportunity presents itself; and if I find that there is one, I must also inquire whether he can be deceitful; for without the knowledge of these two truths, I do not see that I can ever be certain of anything. (p. 115)*

And so Descartes embarks in the remainder of *Meditation 3* on a proof of the existence of God. His thought here is that if he can establish the existence of an all-good and all-powerful God, then he can eliminate the possibility that he is being radically deceived. This is because an all-good and powerful God wouldn't create man with such a deceptive nature and wouldn't deceive us either. For, according to Descartes, deception is a mark of weakness or evil. So, if God exists, then the idea of a deceiving demon no longer holds force and all clear and distinct ideas can be taken as reliable. So proving God's existence becomes a way of guaranteeing that the foundations of Descartes' new system of knowledge – his clear and distinct beliefs – really are true.

■ **Figure 7.2**
God is the guarantor of the truth of beliefs I clearly and distinctly perceive to be true.

Clear and distinct ideas: the foundations of knowledge

GOD

The Trademark Argument for the existence of God

Read *Meditation 3* paragraphs 6–27

Descartes' so-called 'Trademark' Argument for the existence of God involves some complicated and outdated philosophical vocabulary and it takes place over several fairly densely argued pages of *Meditation 3*. If you are relatively new to philosophy this can make his reasoning very difficult to follow by simply reading the text unaided. Despite this, the fundamental idea behind the argument is fairly straightforward, and it will be useful to have a sense of what the argument is trying to achieve before actually tackling Descartes' exposition of it.

The basic point of the argument is to try to show that Descartes' idea of God can only have appeared in his mind if there really is a God. Much like the trademark on a piece of clothing reveals the maker, so the idea of God within his mind reveals its maker, namely God himself. To show this, Descartes argues that the idea of an infinite being (i.e. God) cannot be produced from within the mind of a finite being like himself or anyone else. The cause of such an idea, he argues, can only be a being which really is infinite.

Here is an outline of the argument which follows its development through the text. If you read the summary of each point, then read what Descartes has to say, you should be able to follow the development of his thought.

An outline of the Trademark Argument

1 I know that ideas exist in my mind, but I don't know whether what they represent really exists outside of my mind (pp. 115–16).

2 I am led to think that my ideas of material things represent real physical things, but this judgement is made by a 'blind and rash impulse; not by the natural light of reason' (p. 118).

3 So can I prove there is anything outside of my mind (p. 118)?

4 Yes. My ideas have degrees of 'objective reality', that is to say, what they represent can be thought of as being more or less 'perfect'. For example, my idea of a *mode* is less perfect than my idea of a *substance*, which in turn is less perfect than my idea of *God* (p. 119).

5 '[T]here must be at least as much reality in the efficient and total cause as in its effect.' In other words, any effect cannot be greater than what caused it: it cannot be more 'perfect' or contain more 'reality' than its effect (p. 119). (We will call this Descartes' *causal principle*.)

6 It follows that, since our ideas must come from somewhere and so must be caused by something, their causes must contain at least as much reality or perfection as the ideas themselves (pp. 119–121).

7 So if I can be sure that I cannot be the cause of one of my ideas, then I shall know that there must be something other than me in the world (p. 121).

8 Now, I could well be the cause of my idea of physical substances (e.g. a goat, a rock or a tree) since I am myself a substance (i.e. a thinking substance). I may not be aware that I am the origin of such ideas, but then it is quite possible that perceptions come from some unknown part of me. So I cannot prove that physical things really exist outside my mind (pp. 121–3).

9 But what of God? My idea of God is that of an 'infinite substance' with 'great attributes'. Since I am only a finite substance (which I must be since I make mistakes), I am not sufficiently perfect to create this idea myself. So I cannot be the cause of my idea of God (pp. 123–4).

10 Since the cause of my idea of God must be at least as perfect as the idea, the only thing that can be the cause of it is God himself.

And so it follows that God exists.

ACTIVITY Read through *Meditation 3* and identify where each of the above premises can be found in the text.

Here is a formal version of the essential steps of the argument.

Premise 1 The cause of anything must be at least as perfect as its effect.
Premise 2 My ideas must be caused by something.
Premise 3 I am an imperfect being.
Premise 4 I have the idea of God, which is that of a perfect being.
Intermediate conclusion 1
   I cannot be the cause of my idea of God.
Intermediate conclusion 2
   Only a perfect being (i.e. God) can be the cause of my idea of God.
Main conclusion God must exist.

■ Figure 7.3

Descartes is moving from knowledge of his idea of God in his mind, to the cause of that idea outside of his mind. This cause must be God, and so God must exist.

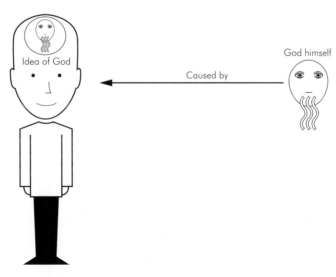

Idea of God

God himself

Caused by

Interpretation of the argument

more difficult

Having tackled Descartes' text you may feel rather confused about the details of his argument and in this section we will work through the argument in greater depth to try to clarify some of the intricacies. However, if you grasp the outline versions above, you have understood the main ideas.

■ Ideas and sensations are like pictures: they have 'representational content'

Descartes' argument for the existence of God has to begin by looking into his own mind and the thoughts it contains. This is because at present all he can be certain of, as we have seen, is the existence of his own thoughts and experiences. As he begins this examination he observes that:

Among my thoughts, some are, as it were, the images of things, and it is to these alone that the name idea properly belongs; as when I represent to myself a man, a chimera, the sky, an angel or God himself. (p. 115)

What Descartes is saying is that some of his thoughts – what he terms 'ideas' – are a bit like pictures or images, in that they seem to represent things. For example, if I think of a goat or Jupiter, my idea is a kind of picture of a goat or Jupiter. And this is true whether or not such things actually exist outside of my mind. So even though a chimera (a mythical creature) doesn't exist I can still have the idea or image of it in my mind.

Similarly, my sensations appear to represent objects outside of me. They too seem to picture something beyond themselves. They too are like images. Another way of expressing this point is to say that ideas and sensations have 'representational content'.

■ Ideas and sensations cannot be false

But, as we have seen, often my ideas and sensations do not accurately represent things outside of me and I can make mistakes. It may even be that there is *nothing* outside of me, and all my ideas and sensations represent nothing in reality at all; they only seem to. But, even if this were true, ideas and sensations *in themselves* cannot strictly be termed 'false', only the *judgement* made on their basis concerning the nature of things outside of me. So, as long as I confine myself to ideas, as they appear in the mind, without making any judgements about what is outside of me, I cannot go wrong.

Now, concerning ideas, if they are considered only in themselves, and are not referred to any other thing, they cannot, strictly speaking, be false; for whether I imagine a goat or a chimera, it is no less true that I imagine the one than the other. (p. 116)

So, to clarify again, his point here is that whatever the real world turns out to be like, and whether it exists or not, my ideas are real and I can't be mistaken about what they are like. Mistakes can *only* creep in once I make *judgements* about the world beyond my mind. The judgement that sensations and ideas resemble and are caused by physical objects is subject to error, but the sensations and ideas considered in themselves are not. So while sensations are not subject to our will, in other words we can't control what we see, hear or smell, this doesn't show that they must come from outside of us. They could be produced from some part of ourselves of which we are unaware, as they seem to be in dreams.

■ Only the clearly and distinctly perceived properties are likely actually to exist

At this point Descartes makes an observation which will be important later in *Meditation 6* when he is concerned to prove that physical objects exist but which is not crucial to the present argument. He reminds us that we discovered with the wax that perceptible qualities such as colour, sound and odour are experienced in what he calls a 'confused' and 'obscure' way, while those of magnitude, substance, motion, duration, etc. (i.e. intelligible ideas) are clear and distinct. And so, argues Descartes, these latter qualities may really exist in objects, if, that is, objects do actually exist. His reasoning here is that because sensation is 'confused' we cannot know what sort of thing it might represent in the physical world, if anything. What he means by this is that we can't tell simply by examining our experience what may have caused it.

… the ideas I have of cold and heat are so unclear and indistinct that I cannot discern from them if cold is only a privation of heat, or if heat is a privation of cold; or if they are both real qualities or not. (p. 122)

So from my experience of heat I can't tell what kind of a thing causes me to feel it. Similarly, when I sense red or smell chocolate I cannot tell what kind of a thing in the world might be causing such sensations. I can form no clear answer to the question of what it is about chocolate that makes it taste chocolatey.

But when it comes to sizes, shapes, etc., I *can* tell what kind of a thing might be causing me to have such sense experiences. If I see something square, I know what kind of a thing in the world might cause this experience, namely something square. So as far as the clear and distinct ideas he has of CORPOREAL things are concerned, it is at least conceivable that they accurately represent real qualities of objects (although, of course, this is yet to be established since there is nothing about these ideas which means that they cannot have been produced by myself).

Here Descartes is clearly alluding to the primary/secondary quality distinction. Whether or not the world exists, my perceptions of secondary qualities must be inaccurate in their representation of reality. They don't have any clear representational content; that is, I have no idea what being red really amounts to for an object. However, my perceptions of primary qualities do have clear representational content. I know exactly what they picture. Part of Descartes' idea here is that the primary qualities lend themselves to geometric description and so can be clearly and distinctly grasped by the understanding. This suggests that they may actually be real. Our sensations of colour, smell, sound, and so on cannot be described in the clear and distinct language of geometry, and so cannot be grasped by the intellect and so cannot be real. This claim needs also to be read in the light of his observations about the wax, namely that its essence is intuited by the mind. This essence is describable in geometry: it is extended and malleable. The outer clothing of the wax is apprehended only confusedly by the senses.

experimenting with ideas

Opposite are some of the physical objects that Descartes mentions perceiving in the *Meditations*. Which can his intellect make sense of so that he can recognise what it would be for the object to possess this quality in reality? Which, in other words, of the perceived qualities of these objects would he claim to perceive clearly and distinctly? By contrast, which qualities does he perceive only in an unclear and indistinct way? In other words, which is his intellect unable to fathom and so cannot know what it is in the world which might be causing such perceptions?

Object	Ideas that Descartes forms from encountering the object	Do these ideas represent a 'real quality' of the object? (yes or no)
The sun	Yellow	
	Hot	
	Small	
	Far away	
A piece of wax	Cylindrical	
	Malleable	
	Light	
	Smooth	
The fire	Hot	
	Bright	
	In front of him	
	Yellow	
His body	Hungry	
	Made of flesh and bones	
	Bearded	
	Naked in bed	

■ Ideas have differing degrees of 'objective reality'[25]

Returning now to the main thrust of the Trademark Argument, what all this amounts to is that so far Descartes has failed to detect anything in my mental life to establish the existence of anything beyond the mind. In particular, it would seem that the cause of my sensations of physical things could be lurking in my unconscious. I may be dreaming after all; there could be some evil demon, mad scientist, or something more sinister planting sense experiences into my mind.

Despite this, Descartes now claims that not all ideas are on a par, for they can represent very different sorts of thing. In other words, they do have different representational contents.

... those that represent substances are undoubtedly something more and contain in themselves, so to speak, more objective reality, that is to say participate through representation in a higher degree of being or of perfection, than those which represent to me only modes or accidents. Moreover, the idea by which I conceive a God who is sovereign, eternal, infinite, unchangeable, all-knowing, all-powerful and universal Creator of all things outside himself, that idea, I say, has certainly more objective reality in it than those by which finite substances are represented to me. (p. 119)

Here Descartes talks about our ideas having degrees of OBJECTIVE REALITY. He means that whatever our ideas represent (their representational content) can be more or less perfect: the more perfect the thing which some idea represents, the more *objective reality* it possesses.

To get a sense of what this odd way of talking amounts to, take for example the idea of an angel. Descartes reckons such an idea is more perfect than the idea of a goat, and so the angel has more objective reality than the goat. Descartes tells us that our ideas of substances have more objective reality than our ideas of modes, since, if either exists beyond my mind, modes must depend on substances for their existence and so are less perfect than substances. Now, our idea of God, claims Descartes, has the highest degree of objective reality, since it represents the greatest possible being and (if he exists) all other beings depend on him for their existence.

So here Descartes has introduced a kind of hierarchy among our ideas. How high an idea sits in terms of its degree of objective reality depends on where what it represents would sit in terms of its dependence on other things or its degree of perfection. Descartes uses the terms 'formal' or 'actual' reality to denote the degree of perfection possessed by actual things, rather than ideas. So we can say of actual substances that they have more FORMAL REALITY than modes, just as our ideas of substances have more objective reality than our ideas of modes.

■ **Figure 7.4**
Descartes' hierarchy of ideas

Descartes produces a hierarchy amongst ideas depending on how much 'objective reality' they possess. At the top is our idea of God. At the bottom are ideas of accidents. The rationale for the hierarchy is that ideas lower down on the list represent things that depend for their existence on things higher up on the list. This is not to say, yet, that any of these things really exist, just that the ideas' representational contents have such dependency relations. In Descartes' terminology their formal (or actual) reality can be ranked in this way.

Ideas		What they represent	
Idea of God	High degree of objective reality	God	High degree of formal reality
Idea of angels		Angels	
Idea of humans		Humans	
Ideas of substances		Substances	
Ideas of modes		Modes	
Ideas of accidents	Low degree of objective reality	Accidents	Low degree of formal reality

The causal principle

Descartes now introduces a general principle which he thinks is self-evident. He writes:

Now it is manifest by the natural light that there must be at least as much reality in the efficient and total cause as in its effect. (p. 119)

What Descartes is saying here is that the cause of anything must, in some sense, be *adequate* to its effect. So, you can't cause something to happen unless the cause is sufficient to make the effect. A corollary of this principle is that 'nothingness cannot produce anything' (p. 119). The thought here is plausible enough: if something occurs, what caused it has to have enough power or *oomph*, as it were, to produce the effect.

To illustrate the basic idea, imagine that a window shatters. Now, we can tell that whatever caused it to shatter must have had enough power – what Descartes here calls 'reality' – to make it shatter. So, it couldn't have been shattered by something too small or weak, such as a grain of sand or a fly. It would have to have been something big and powerful enough, or with sufficient 'reality', or *oomph*, such as a brick or a goat.

Descartes gives us his own example to illustrate his point. He asks us to consider the production of a stone. Whatever it was that caused a stone to come into existence would have to be sufficient to have produced it. This means that the stone cannot come into existence 'unless it be produced by something which has ... everything that enters into the composition of a stone, in other words which contains in itself the same properties as those in the stone, or others superior to them' (p. 119). Similarly something cannot be made hot, Descartes claims, unless it is caused to do so by something 'which is of an order, degree or kind, at least as perfect as heat' (p. 120).[26]

What must have caused my ideas?

Armed with his causal principle Descartes now proceeds to consider the possible causes of his various ideas and of their degree of objective reality. Our ideas, after all, must be caused by something, and the causal principle suggests to Descartes that this cause will have to have at least as much reality as the ideas. In other words our ideas cannot be more perfect or have more objective reality than what has caused them.

Now, in order that an idea may contain one particular objective reality rather than another, it must undoubtedly receive it from some cause, in which is to be found at least as much formal reality as this idea contains objective reality. For if we suppose that something is to be found in the idea which is not to be found in its cause this must then come from nothing. (p. 120)

So it seems clear to Descartes that the objective reality of his ideas can only be caused by something with sufficient formal reality to produce that level of objective reality. So this gives Descartes a way of trying to prove that something other than himself exists. For:

if the objective reality of any one of my ideas is such that I know clearly that it is not within me, ... and that consequently I cannot myself be its cause, it follows necessarily from this that I am not alone in the world, but that there is besides some other being who exists, and who is the cause of this idea. (p. 121)

In other words, if he can show that he does not have the wherewithal within himself to produce one of the ideas he has, then this idea will have to have been caused by something else. And if this can be shown, Descartes will finally have established that he is not alone.

■ **Figure 7.5**
Descartes' causal principle

Descartes' causal principle says that the cause of anything must be sufficient to produce the effect. Since ideas must be caused by something, if Descartes can show that he is not himself sufficient to produce them, this will show that something else must have caused them. And this means that something other than himself must exist.

Ideas in the mind

Where do my ideas come from? If I could not have made them up myself, they must have come from outside of me.

How does the casual principle apply to Descartes' hierarchy of ideas? Descartes argues that his ideas of humans, animals or angels could be made up by himself out of his ideas of material things and of his idea of God, even if these things didn't exist. The thought here is that, so long as he has an idea of physical things, he can make up men and animals in his imagination, just as we make up the idea of a unicorn. The idea of angels, although far greater things than that of humans, is lesser than his idea of God, and so could be invented as lesser versions of God. Moreover, the idea of physical things themselves could also be invented. For there is no reason to think that he, being himself a thinking substance, couldn't be the cause of the idea of physical substances. So it is quite possible that perceptions come from some unknown part of himself. So he cannot prove that physical things really exist (pp. 121–3).

ACTIVITY   Descartes claims to have a very clear and distinct idea of God, and of the qualities or attributes that he possesses. Before we look at Descartes' idea, consider your own idea of God.

List the main qualities or attributes that you think God possesses. Note that this should be possible whether or not you believe God exists. All you are doing is analysing your idea or concept of God.

This just leaves Descartes' idea of God, i.e. the idea of:

an infinite substance, Eternal, IMMUTABLE, independent, omniscient, omnipotent, and by which I and all the other things which exist (if it be true that any such exist) have been created and produced. (pp. 123–4)

Descartes reckons that the attributes of God:

are so great and eminent, that the more attentively I consider them, the less I am persuaded that the idea I have of them can originate in me alone. And consequently I must necessarily conclude from all I have said hitherto, that God exists; for, although the idea of substance is in me, for the very reason that I am a substance, I would not, nevertheless, have the idea of an infinite substance, since I am a finite being, unless the idea had been put into me by some substance which was truly infinite. (p. 124)

What Descartes is saying here is that, since the cause of my idea of God must have at least as much formal reality as the idea has objective reality, the only thing that can be the cause of it is God himself. For the idea of an infinite substance could not have originated from within me who is only a finite substance. The only cause with sufficient reality to produce the idea of an *infinite* being would have to be an infinite being. It follows that the idea of God must have been planted in me by God himself, and so God must exist.

Moreover, Descartes elaborates, the notion of the infinite must precede that of the finite (i.e. the notion of God must precede that of myself) since the latter could only be recognised by contrasting it to the former (p. 124). Thus the idea I have of God:

. . . was born and produced with me at the moment of my creation. And, in truth, it should not be thought strange that God, in creating me, should have put in me this idea to serve, as it were, as the mark that the workman imprints on his work. (p. 130)

In other words, his idea of God is *innate*.

We have followed Descartes through some fairly complex reasoning, and it will not be surprising if you have found it difficult to follow. However, remember there are two summaries on pages 88 and 89 above which should give you a feel of the overall thrust of his thinking. Having made the effort to make sense of what he is trying to say, you may have your suspicions that, despite the complex language, there are some fairly obvious difficulties with Descartes' thinking.

ACTIVITY   Before turning to an evaluation of his argument below, look again at the outline of the main steps of the argument (see pp. 88–9 of this book), and see whether any of them strike you as implausible. Try to explain what you think is wrong with them and make a note of your objections.

Evaluation of the Trademark Argument

■ The Cartesian Circle

▶ criticism ◀   This criticism concerns the overall form of Descartes' strategy in the *Meditations* rather than taking issue with any particular step in this argument for God's existence, and so we need to begin by recalling where we have got to. Recall first the Evil Demon Hypothesis of *Meditation 1*. Descartes needs to dispel the possibility that he could be being radically deceived by such a demon and to this end he is trying to establish that all clear and distinct ideas are reliable guides to the truth. To show that this is the case for certain, Descartes needs to establish the existence of an all-good and all-powerful God, since such a being would not allow him to be deceived in this way about things that seem so self-evident. And this is why he embarks on the Trademark Argument.

But until the proof of God's existence is complete, the possibility that the demon is deceiving him has not been eliminated. So if the demon does exist, then couldn't he fool Descartes into thinking that he had proved the existence of God when in fact he hadn't? If you weren't persuaded by the argument, you might well have thought that Descartes was duped – if not by an evil demon then by the prejudices of his upbringing – into thinking that such an argument could prove the existence of God. So how can he be so sure that somewhere in all this reasoning he hasn't made a mistake? It is certainly not obvious that none is possible, and if we take seriously the possibility that he could be mistaken when counting the sides of a square or adding 2 and 3, then how much more probable is it that he has made a mistake here?

Take as an example the causal principle that 'there must be at least as much reality in the efficient and total cause as in its effect' (p. 119). This is crucial to Descartes' argument and Descartes takes this to be clearly and distinctly knowable. Now, quite apart from whether it really *is* obviously true, the fact that he hasn't yet dismissed the demon possibility means it is still possible for the demon to deceive him into thinking it is true when it isn't.

Descartes' reasoning here appears to be circular, i.e. it presupposes what it sets out to prove. He wants to prove that judgements he understands clearly and distinctly must be true and to do this he needs to prove God's existence. Yet the argument he uses to prove God's existence depends upon the truth of the judgements made in its construction. So until Descartes has proved that these judgements are reliable he cannot prove God exists, and he cannot prove God exists until he knows these judgements are reliable. Descartes' whole enterprise seems to have stalled: caught in the double bind known as the CARTESIAN CIRCLE.

■ **Figure 7.6 The Cartesian Circle**

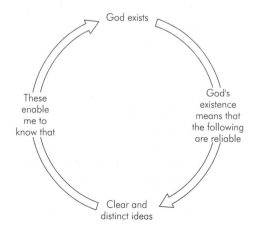

God exists

These enable me to know that

God's existence means that the following are reliable

Clear and distinct ideas

A more familiar example of such a circular justification occurs in the following chain of reasoning:

Q How do you know that God exists?
A *Because it says so in the Bible.*
Q How do you know what the Bible says is true?
A *Because it's the word of God.*

We could construct a similar line of reasoning from the above passage of the *Meditations.*

Q How do you know that God exists?
A *Because I proved his existence using clear and distinct ideas.*
Q How do you know that clear and distinct ideas are reliable?
A *Because a non-deceiving God exists.*

This criticism was levelled at Descartes' *Meditations* soon after they were written, and so Descartes had the opportunity to reply to it. What Descartes needs is a way of establishing the reliability of clear and distinct ideas which doesn't rely on clear and distinct ideas in the first place. We will return to this key difficulty on page 120 and consider Descartes' response.

■ Is the causal principle true?

▶ criticism ◀ Descartes' causal principle states that 'there must be at least as much reality in the efficient and total cause as in its effect' (p. 119). Descartes clearly believes this is self-evidently true. Part of his thinking is that you cannot get more out of the effect than was already in the cause, otherwise you would be getting something for nothing. Since it is self-evident that nothing can come from nothing, this must be impossible. However, when looking at the world, there do – on the face of it at least – appear to be all kinds of examples where it does seem possible to produce something with more perfection or reality than there was originally in its cause. Can we not light a bonfire with a match? Or cause an avalanche with a whisper? Here the causes appear to have markedly *less* reality than what they are able to produce. Chaos theory also suggests that great effects can follow from small causes, as in the well-known example of a butterfly's wing-flap setting in motion a chain of events leading to a hurricane. Consider also the effects of a long process such as evolution. Incremental changes over billions of years can produce complex creatures such as ourselves out of disorganised matter. Here the effect surely has vastly more 'perfection' than the original cause. Quantum physics may also be cited as evidence against Descartes' principle, with its denial of the principle that all events have causes which are adequate to them. If these are true counter-examples to Descartes' causal principle then the Trademark Argument cannot rely on it, and it may well be possible to produce the idea of God from pretty humble beginnings. Below we will consider some ways in which this might happen.

■ Hume on causation

▶ criticism ◀ David Hume famously argued that we cannot determine the cause of anything simply by examining the effect and in so doing is effectively attacking Descartes' causal principle. If I see a window break I cannot deduce what kind of thing must have caused it. We said earlier that we can know that something big enough to have broken it must have impacted with the pane of glass, but how do we know this? Not by reasoning *a priori*, claims Hume, but rather by reference to our past experience of shattering glass. We have learned exclusively from experience which kinds of things can succeed in breaking windows; and if we were to encounter a window breaking for the first time, we would have no idea what caused it. I can only learn that cold weather causes water to freeze by observing water freezing in cold weather. I cannot deduce it *a priori* from observing a puddle of water and thinking very hard about what might happen if the temperature drops.

So the only way we can tell what the cause of something is, Hume says, is by observing it in conjunction with its effect. If he is right, then it seems to follow that, by simple consideration of my idea of God, I cannot know what must have caused it. To find out, I would have to observe its coming into existence.

■ Reality doesn't admit of degrees

▶ criticism ◀ The great English philosophical contemporary of Descartes, and the author of the second objections to the *Meditations*, Thomas Hobbes, argued that the notion of 'degrees of reality' makes no sense. He asks 'Does reality admit of more or less? Or does he [Descartes] think one thing can be more of a thing than another?'[27] Hobbes is saying that things either exist or they don't. One thing or idea cannot have more 'reality' than another, so the whole idea of a hierarchy among our ideas is a nonsense.

Compare the idea you had of God (activity on page 97) with Descartes' idea of God (page 97).

a) In what ways, or in what qualities, does your idea of God differ from Descartes' idea?

b) If your idea of God does differ from Descartes' idea, what implications might this have for Descartes' Trademark Argument? Is it important for Descartes' argument that everyone has the same idea of God?

■ Do we really have an idea of an infinite being?

▶ criticism ◀ A premise of Descartes' argument is that he has the idea of God: 'the idea by which I conceive a God who is sovereign, eternal, infinite, unchangeable, all-knowing, all-powerful and universal Creator of all things outside himself' (p. 119). But can we really grasp such an idea? Even good theistic philosophers have expressed doubts about whether the human mind can actually frame a positive idea of God because of our imperfection and finitude.[28] He may be just too great for us to understand. So it can be argued that Descartes is able to use the word 'God' without having a genuine corresponding idea in his mind. The idea of an infinite being, like that of infinity, may be something we can express in words but not truly understand. If I try to conceive of infinity my mind fails me; the idea is really only a negative one: the opposite of finite. Now if this is right, and we don't really have the idea of an infinite being, then the issue of where the idea comes from doesn't arise, and so the Trademark Argument doesn't get off the ground.

■ The idea of God is incoherent

▶ criticism ◀ Another reason for thinking that we don't have a proper idea of God in the first place is that it is contradictory. Note that, in his account of his idea of God, Descartes says that God is all-powerful. If this is right then what is the answer to the question of whether God can set himself a task that he cannot perform? If he *can*, then there is a task he cannot perform; and if he *cannot* there is a task he cannot perform (namely set himself a task that he cannot perform) and so either way he cannot be all-powerful. This paradox in the very notion of omnipotence suggests that Descartes' idea of God is confused; and clearly the cause of a confused idea need not be that great, and certainly need not be caused by God himself. It would be far more likely to have originated within Descartes himself as just another example of his faulty thinking.

ACTIVITY | Descartes has an idea of God as an infinite, supremely intelligent, supremely powerful, creator of the world. List all the possible causes of these ideas – where might Descartes (or any other believer) have got these ideas from?

■ The origins of the idea of an all-powerful God are contingent

► criticism ◄ It often occurs to those encountering this argument for the first time to point out that people from other religions don't have an idea of an all-powerful God. And if they don't have such an idea then Descartes is surely wrong to say that it is planted in our minds. Similarly, it can be argued on empirical grounds that we know that the origin of the idea of an omnipotent God is not divine since it has a historical genesis around 500 BC in Palestine. We can imagine how the idea of an all-powerful being came about, as competing tribes each claimed their own god to be more powerful than those of the others. Eventually one tribe hit upon the idea that their own god was *all-powerful,* thereby trumping the competition. Having an *all*-powerful God means that no other tribe can ever again claim to have a god more powerful still. This is a great idea, but one of human – all too human – origin.

Now Descartes would not be overly impressed by such an argument as he can explain how it can be that people don't always appear to have the idea of God, even though it is innate. For all this shows is that people don't always think hard enough about metaphysical issues. Compare this with mathematics where we often fail to learn many of its truths, and yet these truths are still universal and innate. We can point to the historical discovery of *pi* but this doesn't mean that it is not a universal constant discoverable *a priori.* Nonetheless, if we put this objection next to our questioning of the causal principle above, it does give us an alternative account of how such an idea might evolve from origins far less than divine.

■ Empiricist accounts of the origin of our idea of God

► criticism ◄ Empiricists argue that all our concepts come from experience, and so have an account of how we can generate the idea of God from experience. The basic idea, argued for by Hume among others, is that we can observe the relative virtues in other people, and so recognise that there are degrees of goodness, or power, or wisdom. Having observed this, we can imagine extending the degree of such virtues indefinitely until we reach the idea of infinite goodness, infinite power or infinite wisdom. In this way we arrive at the idea of an infinite being, perfect in every way, but the cause of the idea is not in the least infinite or perfect.

The Contingency Argument

> **Read** Meditation 3
> paragraphs 28–end

Descartes now produces what appears to be a second argument for God's existence. He now asks whether the fact of his own existence is enough to show that there must be a God (p. 126). To answer this he investigates where his own existence might have come from. The possibilities that suggest themselves are that he created himself, that his parents or some other cause less perfect than God created him, or that God created him. So he considers these possibilities in turn.

■ Does my existence derive from myself?

Descartes reasons that if he were the author of his own being, and so depended on nothing else for his existence, then he would have made himself perfect and so he would be God. But clearly he is not God since he has so many imperfections – for example he doesn't know everything, as is shown from the fact that he doubts so much – and so he cannot have created himself (p. 127).

■ Have I always existed?

So is it possible that he has always existed? Descartes answers that, even if he had, this would not mean that he was himself the author of his own being, for since his past existence is not sufficient to guarantee his present existence, there must also be something which *conserves* his existence at every moment. Now, clearly he doesn't conserve *himself* in existence since if he did, as a conscious being, he would be aware of this. So it follows that he must be conserved by something other than himself (p. 128) and which is the ultimate explanation for his existence.

■ Does my existence derive from my parents?

Could his parents or some other cause less great than God be the author of his being? Well, in some sense, of course they are, since it is because of them that he was born. But, for Descartes, his parents do not create him out of nothing; they are simply the occasion of a certain organisation of the matter of which he is composed. Nor do they conserve him in his existence and so they cannot be the ultimate explanation for his existence. Moreover, looking to his parents doesn't provide any ultimate explanation for his existence since we are now left with the question of where they derived their existence, and so we end up in an infinite regress.

■ Does my existence derive from God?

Since Descartes and his parents (or any similar imperfect cause) have been rejected and there must be an ultimate cause for his existence we have to suppose God to be the ultimate explanation. For, since, as we have seen, 'there must be at least as much reality in the cause as in the effect' and since he is a thinking thing, he must be caused by something with at least as much reality as a thinking substance. And, in Descartes' terminology, that substance must contain formally the perfections that his idea of God possesses objectively. Now although his physical being may have come from his parents, his conscious being as a thinking substance can only have come from another thinking substance. Thus, Descartes can conclude that God exists.

Here is an outline of the argument:

What is the cause of my existence as a thinking thing? Is it:
a) myself, b) I have always existed, c) my parents, or d) God?

a) I cannot have caused myself to exist for then I would have created myself perfect. Nor can I sustain myself in existence for then I would be God.
b) Neither have I always existed for then I would be aware of this.
c) My parents may be the cause of my physical existence but not of me as a thinking mind.
d) Therefore, only God could have created me.

ACTIVITY   Does this argument strike you as a sound one? If not, which of the premises would you say are suspect; and/or which step would you say wasn't justified?

Interpretation and evaluation

■ Could I not be what created and conserves me?

► criticism ◄ We might object that even though Descartes is not aware of having the power to sustain himself in existence, he might nonetheless have it. Descartes' response would doubtless be that if as a conscious being he were always conserving his own existence he could not but be conscious of this activity going on within himself. So, if he is not conscious of the activity which preserves him, he cannot be its author. Nonetheless, this defence is not particularly convincing since Descartes has accepted that dreams have a cause of which we are not conscious and yet which may come from within us, and so it seems possible that we may have aspects to our own nature of which we are unaware. Moreover, we are supposing that at this stage Descartes has not established that he is nothing more than a thinking substance. In other words, not until *Meditation 6* does he claim to have proven that his essence is pure thought, and that he is definitely a distinct substance from his body. But until he has proven this, he cannot be certain that his brain or his body generally is what sustains and produces his consciousness. If I am my body, then there may well be physical aspects of myself of which I am unaware and which are the necessary conditions for my existence and continuance in existence.

■ Could we not have been created by a less than perfect being?

► criticism ◄ Could we not have been created by another conscious being less great than God, say an evil scientist or an angel or a demon? Why must our author be a *perfect* thinking being?

Descartes does look at the possibility that we could be put together by a series of less than perfect causes (p. 129). His response to this invokes the original Trademark Argument about the source of his idea of God. He writes:

... the unity, simplicity or inseparability of all the properties of God, is one of the principal perfections that I conceive to be in him; and, indeed, the idea of this unity and assembly of all the perfections of God cannot have been put in me by any cause from which I did not also receive the ideas of all the other perfections. (p. 129)

In other words, if he were created by a being lesser than God, or which was only perfect in some ways, he could not have the idea of a God which is perfect in every way. This suggests that the second argument cannot establish that he is created by a perfect being, but only that he is created by a being with more reality than he has himself, as a thinking thing, but that this could fall short of being God. For this reason the Trademark Argument is the more important one and the Contingency Argument actually relies upon it.

Error and the will

Read *Meditation 4* paragraphs 13–15

Like *Meditation 3*, *Meditation 4* is steeped in much outmoded philosophical terminology and, while significant to Descartes' overall strategy, we can deal with it here more briefly than the other *Meditations* and still retain a good sense of the overall development of Descartes' argument across the whole work.

Having established good reasons for believing that God exists, Descartes hopes now to pass on to knowledge of other things. For having proved God's existence, he now knows he can rely on clear and distinct ideas as a basis for establishing further knowledge. However, in the process of eliminating the possibility of radical doubt, Descartes has left himself with the opposite problem – how is error at all possible? After all, if God is a non-deceiver then, by Descartes' own logic, I should be incapable of making mistakes. Since I obviously am capable of making mistakes, something must have gone wrong with Descartes' reasoning. So why do I make mistakes in the first place? How can Descartes account for the fact of my fallibility?

ACTIVITY   Think about the journey Descartes took to get from the question 'how is knowledge possible?' to the question 'how is error possible?'

a) Write down the main stages of the journey:

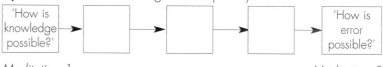

Meditation 1   *Meditation 3*

b) Which stage do you think is the most important?
c) Which stage do you think is most vulnerable to criticism?

Meditation 4 focuses on solving the problem of how to account for our fallibility. Descartes' answer is that our understanding, *properly deployed*, cannot make mistakes.

If I do make errors, therefore, it is only because of making rash judgements. Mistakes occur when I jump to conclusions without having thought things through. They are the consequence of my making judgements on the basis of confused ideas, or ideas that I do not clearly understand. And it is 'the power of choice, or free will' (p. 135) which, by over-reaching itself, enables me to make such judgements. So in order to avoid falsehood I need to restrain the will and avoid my understanding assenting to any judgement which is not based on clearly and distinctly perceived ideas. For example, at the moment I am still unable to determine whether I am in essence a thinking thing, or whether I am actually in some way necessarily bound up with my physical body. Since I cannot yet adjudicate clearly and distinctly on this matter, I must suspend any judgement, and in this way I can avoid falling into error (p. 138).

This means that God has given me the means to correct the errors I make, and so I, not he, am the cause of the errors I do make. He has given me an intellect or understanding which can use reason to discover the truth, and it is down to me if I choose not to use this faculty properly. Since God has given me the means to correct my errors, it is not incompatible with his goodness or power that I should make mistakes. However, it would be incompatible with his nature to make me in such a way that what I understand clearly and distinctly should be mistaken. For in this case I have no way of recognising or correcting this mistake. Such a radical deception, one I have no means of overcoming, would be extreme indeed, and not the kind of thing one would expect an all-good and all-powerful God to impose on one of his creatures.

Interpretation and evaluation

Descartes is saying that, so long as he now proceeds with great care in his investigations, he should be able to avoid making any more mistakes. God is no demon. He would not be so underhand as to deceive Descartes about the things he sees most clearly and distinctly to be true, such as that 2 added to 3 makes 5, or that squares have four sides. The reason he has gone wrong in the past is that he hasn't proceeded by incremental steps which are clearly and distinctly recognised, but rather has allowed himself to rush to conclusions based on insufficient evidence. It is the weaker side of his nature which allows this to happen. But if he restricts himself to what reason and the understanding allow him to conclude, God guarantees that he cannot go wrong. So from now on he must rebuild his body of knowledge exclusively using clear and distinct ideas.

Key points: Chapter 7

What you need to know about *Meditation 3* – the Trademark Argument and *Meditation 4* – error and the will:

1 Descartes asks what it was about the *cogito* that meant he could know it with absolute certainty. He answers that it was that he perceived its truth clearly and distinctly. This suggests to him that he can establish the general rule that all beliefs that he recognises in the same way can also be known to be true.

2 So if all clear and distinctly perceived truths can be known to be true, Descartes can use these as the basis for rebuilding a body of knowledge.

3 However, there is one problem that needs to be resolved before he can begin to do this in earnest. In *Meditation 1* Descartes entertained the possibility that an evil demon might deceive him, even about things he believed he recognised clearly and distinctly. This possibility needs to be dispelled.

4 To this end Descartes decides to attempt to prove the existence of God. For if he can establish the existence of an all-knowing and all-powerful creator of the universe and of himself, then he can be sure that he cannot be mistaken when making judgements that seem so clear and distinct that it is impossible to conceive of them as not true.

5 Descartes' first proof of God's existence is the Trademark Argument. In it he argues for his causal principle that the cause of anything must have at least as much reality as its effect.

6 Since Descartes' ideas must have causes, he can enquire into the cause of his idea of God. And since the cause of his idea must have at least as much reality as the effect, he is able to argue that neither he nor any finite thing could be the cause of his idea of an infinite being, and that only a being which actually is infinite could be the cause.

7 From this it follows that an infinite being must exist, and that he placed the idea of himself within Descartes' mind, much as a tradesman places his mark on an artefact.

8 Descartes supplements the Trademark Argument with the Contingency Argument. He enquires into the possible origins of his own existence, and rejects the possibility that he could have been produced by any imperfect cause, such as himself or his parents. It follows that only a perfect being, or God, can have created him, and so God exists.

9 In establishing that he has been created by a non-deceiving God, Descartes has made a new problem for himself, namely why he is ever allowed to make mistakes. To explain this, he argues that his errors are not the fault of God; for God has given Descartes the means to avoid error if he only makes judgements on the basis of ideas he understands clearly and distinctly. However, he has also given Descartes a free will, and if Descartes chooses to use this freedom to make rash judgements on the basis of ideas he perceives only obscurely or confusedly, then he runs the risk of making mistakes.

10 Since Descartes now knows that clear and distinct judgements are guaranteed to be true, and that he can avoid error by avoiding making any judgements which are not perceived clearly and distinctly, he can now move forward in his programme to rebuild a body of knowledge with confidence.

Meditation 5: The Ontological Argument

Our idea of material things

Read *Meditation 5* paragraphs 1–6

In the fourth *Meditation* Descartes has argued that clear and distinct ideas are the only basis on which to make sound judgements. With this discovery in mind, at the beginning of the fifth he resolves to find out whether any certain judgements can be made regarding material objects. In other words he is turning once more to try to prove the existence of the material world and establish what it is like. In order to do this he begins by analysing his *ideas* of material objects to see what in them he can understand clearly and distinctly, and what is obscure and confused (p. 142). It is important to recognise that, just as with the discussion of the wax in *Meditation 2*, Descartes is not supposing that material objects exist. He is simply looking more closely at their appearance in his mind.

What in matter is perceived clearly and distinctly?

Descartes' analysis of the appearance of matter reveals some properties which can be clearly and distinctly understood, and others which are obscure and confused. As we might expect, the former category consists of extension in three dimensions, motion, duration, number, etc. These ideas are so clear to me, he says, that they appear to be nothing new, but rather the *recollection* of something already known (p. 142); they seem, that is, to be innate. Thus, even if no such qualities exist outside of my thought (i.e. if there is no material world), nonetheless these ideas have 'true and immutable natures' (an essence or form as one might say), which is unchangeable and eternal. Extension (i.e. three-dimensionality), in other words, has specific geometric properties, and the truths that I can discover about it are not invented by me.

Geometry is *a priori*

Moreover, the ideas of the properties of geometric figures cannot derive from sensation, since I can prove things about triangles and other shapes that I have never seen. In other words, geometric truths are knowable *a priori*. They are recognised clearly and distinctly and therefore are guaranteed to be true. And if geometric truths exist prior to my thinking about them they must be independent of me and not mere figments of my thought. They must be, as Descartes puts it, 'something and not a mere nothing', not yet meaning to imply that there must be extended objects which exemplify these geometric truths, but simply that geometry is objective (pp. 142–4).

Interpretation and evaluation

■ Descartes is not yet saying that matter exists

It is important to be clear that this is not yet an argument about the existence of matter, but rather about the *a priority*, or logical independence, of geometric truths from my own thought and from my experience. Descartes is attempting to show that the essence of his *idea* of body (i.e. matter) can be described in geometry and is not dependent on his thinking. However, he is not suggesting that any material objects actually exist outside his thought. This is because (generally speaking) we can discover the essential nature of our idea of something without this implying anything about whether or not it exists. Indeed, this thought was already in evidence in the discussion of the wax, where Descartes tried to strip his idea of matter down to its essentials and found it to contain 'something extended, flexible and malleable' (p. 109). So when Descartes says that such things are recognised clearly and distinctly as true and therefore that they are *something* and not *nothing* he should not be taken to be implying anything more than that the *a priori* is true independently of my thought. Geometric truths are universally and objectively true and do not depend on my having recognised them to be true. The argument *is* however a preliminary to the final argument for the existence of the physical world which occurs in the sixth *Meditation*. There, Descartes will try to show that those properties of matter which we can clearly and distinctly apprehend are the real or *primary* qualities, while those which are only apprehended obscurely and confusedly are the apparent or *secondary* ones. We will, however, postpone a full discussion of the issue until then.

The Ontological Argument

Contemplating an idea can allow one to derive further truths about it

Read *Meditation 5* paragraphs 7–12

Having made these observations about his idea of matter, Descartes now presents his second argument for the existence of God (p. 144ff.). To get his argument going he uses the example just discussed of his idea of matter. Those properties that I clearly and distinctly perceive in my idea of material things, i.e. the geometric properties, are the basis for judgements I know to be true. And when I contemplate these properties further I can generate all kinds of substantive truths about them. For example, when I contemplate the idea of a triangle I can clearly and distinctly perceive that it necessarily contains the idea of its having three sides. Further study reveals that the sum of its internal angles equals the sum of two right angles. What this shows is that by examining one's ideas we can derive further truths which are, as it were, contained in the ideas themselves. Such truths are part of the essence of the original idea.

experimenting with ideas

We can 'unpack' the idea of 'triangle', as Descartes did, in order to reveal further truths about 'triangles'.

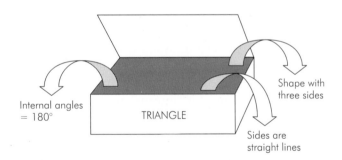

Internal angles = 180°

TRIANGLE

Shape with three sides

Sides are straight lines

Now, unpack each of the following ideas in order to reveal further truths about them. (What are the component ideas that make up each concept?)

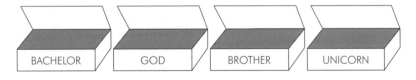

BACHELOR   GOD   BROTHER   UNICORN

Deriving God's existence from my idea of God

Now, it follows that any properties of God that I clearly and distinctly perceive to be part of my idea of him must really be part of the essence of the idea. And if I contemplate my idea of God, I should be able to recognise some further truths about this essence. So what is my idea of God? Well, in essence it is the idea of a supremely perfect being. Now, one property that I perceive as belonging to this nature is existence, and therefore he exists.

■ Is this a trick argument?

Descartes fears that this argument for the existence of God may appear to be 'some kind of logical trick' since the *existence* and *essence* of an object are normally thought to be distinct. In other words, generally speaking, the essential nature of an object, or the idea we have of the nature of something, has no bearing on whether or not it exists. (That Descartes himself generally accepts this principle is shown from the fact that he contemplates the essence of matter, for example in the wax experiment, without supposing that this can establish an answer to the question of whether or not it exists.) So, I can understand that it is part of the essence of a triangle that it must have three sides, but this doesn't tell me anything about whether a triangle actually exists anywhere outside of my mind.

However, Descartes claims, in the case of God things are different. Unlike the case of a triangle, God's existence cannot be distinguished from his essence. For if we try to subtract the property of existence from the idea of God we take away something essential, much as to subtract the property that the sum of its internal angles is equal to two right angles, from the idea of a triangle is to subtract something essential. Thus I cannot think of God as not existing, just as I cannot think of a mountain without a valley (p. 145).

■ But thought cannot impose necessity upon things

Descartes next considers the objection that 'my thought imposes no necessity on things' (p. 145). In other words, I can't make something exist just by thinking about it. So just as 'I can well imagine a winged horse, although there is no such horse, so could I perhaps attribute existence to God, even though no God existed' (p. 145). But, he continues, this objection misses the point that existence in the case of God is essential to the very idea of God, in the same way as a valley is essential to the idea of a mountain. It is not his thought that imposes any necessity on things, but the other way round: it is that fact that the idea of existence is necessarily a part of the idea of God which means Descartes must conceive of God as existing. The idea of a non-existent God would not be an idea of God at all (p. 145).

■ A perfect being must have all perfections

Descartes then elaborates why he believes the very concept of God entails his existence. The idea is that God is the supremely perfect being and a perfect being must be perfect in every way. This means he must be omnipotent (all-powerful), OMNISCIENT (all-knowing), all-good, all-loving, and so on. In other words he must have all perfections. Now, Descartes claims, existence is itself a perfection. That is to say, it is more perfect for something to exist than not to exist. And this means we must include it in the list of perfections possessed by God. And so it follows that God must exist.

■ Descartes' Ontological Argument in outline

Premise 1 I have an idea of God, that is to say, an idea of a perfect being.
Premise 2 A perfect being must have all perfections.
Premise 3 Existence is a perfection.

Conclusion God exists.

ACTIVITY   Most people when they hear this argument are inclined to think that there is something fishy going on. However, it is not obvious what exactly has gone wrong, and it is a controversial matter to identify where the flaw lies – if indeed there is a flaw.
   Before reading on, consider what you think the error Descartes makes here may be. Take note of your thoughts.

Evaluation

■ Gaunilo's objection: 'The perfect island'

▶ criticism ◀   Gaunilo, a monk responding to an earlier version of the Ontological Argument (by St Anselm), argues by modelling Descartes' argument. The argument he gives is this:

Premise 1 I have an idea of a perfect island.
Premise 2 A perfect island must have all perfections.
Premise 3 Existence is a perfection.

Conclusion The perfect island exists.

Gaunilo's point is that, by using Descartes' form of reasoning, we should be able to prove the existence of a perfect anything, such as the perfect island. But obviously it is unlikely that a perfect island does exist, and so it follows that there is something wrong with the reasoning leading to this conclusion. Therefore Descartes' argument cannot work for proving the existence of God.

In response to this, Descartes would probably argue that the idea of God is not like that of an island. Recall that, at the beginning of *Meditation 5*, he likened his idea of God to that of a triangle. Part of his point there was that his ideas of geometric shapes have what he called 'true and immutable natures'. In other words, these ideas have an essence which can be understood by the mind and which is independent of the mind. This is why we can have clear and distinct knowledge of truths about these shapes, for example that the internal angles of a triangle are equal to the sum of two right angles. Now the idea of a perfect island is not like this. It is not an idea we discover within us simply by thinking. It is what we might call a 'made-up' idea in the sense that it depends on our thinking in a way that the idea of a triangle does not. For this reason, what exactly a perfect island would be like is not an objectively discoverable matter that any mind would have to agree on. I cannot simply contemplate the idea of a perfect island and work out what it would have to contain. In fact, its qualities will tend to depend on the particular mind which considers the question and what sorts of things you look for in an island – whether you prefer sunbathing, snorkelling or the nightlife, for example. Now, Descartes claims, the idea of God, the perfect being, is more like that of a triangle, and so we can discover truths about it which are mind independent and discoverable *a priori*.

■ The idea of God is not like that of a triangle

▶ criticism ◀ However, proving that the idea of God really is more like that of a triangle than an island may prove problematic for Descartes. For while there is universal agreement about the meaning of the term 'triangle' and consequently necessary propositions involving the term, this is not so with the concept of God. The concept of God, we can plausibly argue, is vague; there are many different definitions; and much historical disagreement concerning the significance of the term. But if there is no 'true and immutable nature' to the idea, then it looks more like a 'made-up' idea which depends on Descartes' mind for its existence, much like Gaunilo's perfect island. If this is right, then for Descartes to claim he has proved God's existence from his idea is no different from making up the idea of the perfect island, the perfect song or the perfect goat, and demonstrating its existence.

■ Kant's objection: 'Existence is not a predicate'

▶ criticism ◀ Kant's famous criticism of Descartes' version of the Ontological Argument has become the standard objection. Kant argued that Descartes wrongly treats existence as a property or PREDICATE of individuals in the same manner as, for example, a colour can be a property. In other words, Descartes' mistake is to think that existence is a property that we can imagine things as either having or not having, just as we can think of dandelions as being yellow or not being yellow. By treating existence in this way, Descartes is able to argue that existence must be one of the properties or perfections a perfect being would have to have. But there is an important difference between saying that something is yellow and saying that it exists. In the former case I am describing it. To say that dandelions are yellow is to give information about what they are like. To say they exist doesn't tell you anything about what they are like; it merely tells you that there are such things in the world. If I tell you that some cows have horns and some don't, I am telling you about a property possessed by some cows and not by others. But if I tell you that some cows exist and some don't, I seem to be saying something strange precisely because I seem to be implying that there is a property – existence – that some cows have and others don't. But which ones don't? The only answer here is the non-existent ones. But surely there are no non-existent cows, so how can they fail to have a property? Existence cannot be a property that some things don't have, because if they don't exist they don't have any properties at all. And if existence cannot be a property that things can lack, then it cannot be a property that they can have either. Gassendi makes a similar point in his *Objections* (fifth) to the *Meditations* where he says that 'something which does not exist has neither perfection nor imperfection; and what exists and has various perfections, does not have existence as one particular perfection among them – rather, existence is that by which both it and its perfections exist.'

So if existence is not a property it cannot be treated as one of God's perfections alongside omnipotence, omniscience, etc. To say he exists is not to ascribe a property to him, it is to say that there is a God. And if we cannot ascribe existence to God in this way, then it cannot be treated as part of the concept of God.[29]

To help see what Kant means by this, try the following exercise.

1 Imagine your perfect partner/boyfriend/girlfriend.

2 Picture him or her in detail in your head: What does s/he look like? What is her/his personality like? What are her/his hopes and dreams? Write down a short description of your perfect partner, summarising her/his attributes.

3 Now add the following features or *predicates*, one at a time, to your idea of your partner:

- Is lying on a beach in the Caribbean
- Has left you for someone who is much richer and more interesting
- Is now a world-famous film star
- Secretly wants to get back together with you
- Exists.

4 Which of these further predicates changed your image of your perfect partner?

Kant's thought is that only a predicate which makes a difference to our idea of something is a genuine one. But existence doesn't do this. To imagine your partner existing doesn't change the mental picture you have of them in the way that imagining them lying on a beach does. Kant's conclusion is that Descartes' error in the Ontological Argument is to suppose that he can clearly recognise existence to be one of the properties God must have.

■ Caterus' objection: 'Thought cannot impose necessity upon things'

▶ criticism ◀ We saw that Descartes himself considers an objection to his argument: that his thought cannot impose necessity on things. The author of the first set of objections to the *Meditations,* Caterus, thinks Descartes dismisses this objection too quickly. He writes:

Even if it is granted that a supremely perfect being carries the implication of existence in virtue of its very title, it still does not follow that the existence in question is anything actual in the real world; all that follows is that the concept of existence is inseparably linked to the concept of a supreme being.[30]

What Caterus is saying is that if we grant Descartes that the proposition 'God exists' is true by definition, or *analytic,* as philosophers say, it still doesn't actually follow that God exists in reality. All that follows is that the *concept* of existence is contained within the *concept* of God. This can tell us only about definitions or concepts and nothing about reality. In other words it is one thing to talk about the definitions of terms such as 'God' and another to talk about what exists in the world but we can't legitimately move in an argument from the one to the other. So Descartes' idea of God may well involve the idea of a being that exists necessarily. However, while thinking hard about his idea may well reveal this, what it will reveal is only something about the idea, about the meaning of the word 'God', and nothing about whether this word refers to anything beyond itself.

■ In what sense is it more 'perfect' to exist?

► criticism ◄ What is meant by existence being a perfection? We saw when discussing the Trademark Argument that the assumption that we can meaningfully talk about degrees of reality, and the notion that the more perfect something is the more 'real' it is, or the closer it approximates to fullness of being, can be questioned. It certainly doesn't seem to be knowable clearly and distinctly.

God as guarantor of further knowledge

Read *Meditation 5*
paragraphs 13–15

Descartes' arguments for the existence of God are required to progress beyond the confines of his own thinking and to knowledge of other things (p. 148ff.). An important part of this process has been the realisation that a perfect God cannot deceive. This truth, if and when it is perceived, is the most evident of all, and consequently the certainty of everything else depends on it. However, when the mind's eye is not focused on this truth, the reasons for judging it to be true are not kept in view and so can once again be doubted. The certainty of the existence of God, however, guarantees that my memory of having made a clear and distinct argument is accurate. For, if he exists, he will not deceive me in my recollection of what I clearly and distinctly perceived. So I cannot be deceived about what I clearly understand. Thus the awareness of God guarantees certainty in all things that are clearly and distinctly perceived, and particularly those properties of matter which are amenable to mathematical description.

I see clearly that the certainty and truth of all knowledge depends only on the knowledge of the true God in such a way that, before I knew him, I was incapable of knowing anything else perfectly. But now countless things can be known and be certain for me, both about God and other intellectual things, and also about as much of physical nature as falls within the scope of pure mathematics.
(p. 149)

Interpretation and evaluation

■ The Cartesian Circle again

In escaping from doubt Descartes relies on a set of propositions that present themselves to his mind with such force as to be indubitable. These propositions are perceived 'clearly and distinctly' to be true. One example is the *cogito*, another that God is no deceiver. If doubt is to be genuinely defeated, these propositions must actually be true. However, Descartes seems to be saying, the truth of a proposition is not entailed by its being irresistibly believed whenever it is contemplated. For the irresistibility could simply be a matter of psychological compulsion. For this reason Descartes needs to secure knowledge of such propositions by securing the reliability of the intellect when it perceives clearly and distinctly. This reliability is secured by God, for, insofar as he is perfect, we can be sure that he would not deceive us.

▶ criticism ◀ The difficulty that now arises is that the existence of a non-deceiving creator can only be established with certainty *if* we can trust our clear and distinct perception of the Trademark and Ontological Arguments in the first place. For clearly I must rely on my intellect in order to perceive the validity of the proof of God's existence, and the truth of the premises of that proof. Thus it would seem that I need to trust my clear and distinct ideas in order to prove the existence of God; but I also need the existence of God to trust such ideas. This in outline is the problem of the Cartesian Circle. If Descartes has committed a fallacy here his whole enterprise must collapse and he will never be able to escape from the solipsistic confines of the *cogito*.

■ Descartes' defence against charges of circularity

It is perhaps unlikely that Descartes could have been guilty of such an obvious error. One line of defence against the charge of circularity is to claim that there are some propositions of which I can have self-evident knowledge while I am attending them and which do not need the divine guarantee. Specifically, the realisation that a non-deceiving God exists would have to be of this category. This suggests that doubt is not supposed to extend to cover basic intuitions of clearly and distinctly perceived truths. If this is the correct interpretation it may be that Descartes is concerned with guaranteeing his recollection of past steps in a proof, rather than the steps themselves when they are clearly and distinctly being perceived. A belief perceived by a clear and distinct intuition of the mind remains certain only while it is being attended to, thus the veracity of an extended proof would need some guarantee if we are to rely on it. God would, on this interpretation, serve as the guarantor of further knowledge by allowing us to rely on our memory.

Key points: Chapter 8

What you need to know about *Meditation 5* – the Ontological Argument:

1 Descartes points out that, whether or not extended objects exist, we can discover objective truths about them in an *a priori* manner by doing geometry. For example, I can prove truths about a triangle simply by analysing my concept of it. So, if material things exist, there is one property of them, namely their extension in three dimensions, which I can clearly and distinctly understand.
2 Descartes now offers his second main argument for the existence of God, the Ontological Argument. Descartes begins from the fact that he has an idea of God in his mind, and the essence of this idea is of a being which is perfect in every way.
3 Descartes now attempts to show that the idea of existence is necessarily attached to the essence of God, and so demonstrate that it is impossible to conceive of God as not existing, or in other words to show that the claim 'God exists' can be known just by examining the meanings of the words.
4 To this end he argues that it is part of the idea of a perfect being that it have all perfections. Such perfections will include being omniscient, omnipotent, and so on.
5 Existence is also a perfection, since it is more perfect to exist than not to exist, and it follows, therefore, that God necessarily has existence as part of his essence and so he exists.

Meditation 6: The proof of the existence of matter; Cartesian dualism

The sixth *Meditation* draws together many of the threads of the earlier *Meditations.* In it Descartes makes good the move beyond the subjective realm of his own thought and establishes that sense experience is caused by a world of physical objects impacting on the sense organs of his body. He also concludes his argument for the 'real distinctness' of mind and body which began in the second *Meditation*, and discusses the nature of the union of these two substances. Finally he discusses the nature of material reality.

Imagination and intellect

Read *Meditation 6 paragraphs 1–4*

Descartes begins the *Meditation* by returning to a topic we discussed earlier when examining his experiment with the wax, namely the different faculties of his mind: the imagination and the intellect or understanding.

The distinction between the imagination and the intellect or understanding

We have seen that some of the properties of matter are clearly and distinctly perceived, namely those amenable to mathematical and geometric description, and Descartes thinks this means they may actually exist in objects themselves. For, in contrast to our confused ideas of colour, smell and so forth, we know what such properties would represent in reality. In other words, I have a clear idea of what it would be for something to be square or spherical in itself, independently of my perception of it. But, by contrast, I have no real idea of what it is for something to be red, or hot. My perception of red could be caused by anything and I cannot work out what kind of thing it is to be red, just by analysing my idea of red. (Note that this is a point Descartes made earlier, in *Meditation 3*, and which we discussed on page 91 of this book under the heading 'Only the clearly and distinctly perceived properties are likely actually to exist'.)

However, in order to assess whether clearly and distinctly perceived properties actually *do* represent something which exists, Descartes begins by further analysing the natures of the intellect and the imagination. He observes that although I can imagine a triangle – I can, that is, visualise it in my mind – I cannot really imagine a chiliagon (a 1,000-sided figure), for the image I may conjure of the chiliagon is rather hazy and confused and indistinguishable from the image of a myriogon (a 10,000-sided figure) or some other many-sided shape. But this does not mean that the intellect understands the essential nature of a chiliagon any less than that of a triangle: I understand perfectly well what a thousand-sided shape is in the same way as I understand what a three-sided shape is. Descartes concludes that the imagination is a distinct faculty from the intellect, with distinct capacities.

Imagination is inessential to me

But the imagination is not only distinct from the intellect, it is not essential to my nature since I would be the same mind without it (p. 151). Descartes' thought here seems to be that I could still establish my own existence as a thinking thing, that is to say perform the *cogito,* whether or not I were able to conjure up images of material things in my mind's eye. In other words, if I did not have any imagination, I would still be able to think and to reason and still be aware of my own existence as a conscious thing. Descartes concludes from this that the imagination must depend on some object other than the self. His reasoning here is simply that any property of something which does not derive from its own (essential) nature must derive from something else.

What then might be the origin of imagination? Descartes puts forward a plausible idea based on what he used to believe before he began his sceptical meditations, namely that his mind is able to contemplate a body to which it is joined. Perhaps this is how physical objects are imagined. Thus the *imagination* would consist in the mind turning towards the body and apprehending resemblances of things perceived by the senses; while the *intellect* would simply consist in the mind turning towards itself. While the imagination deals with images of material things, the intellect is purely intellectual, dealing with *a priori* truths which require no empirical input.

■ **Figure 9.1**

The intellect is the essential core of the mind. Imagination is inessential, meaning I would be the same mind without it. Our capacity to imagine material things comes from sensation. So where does sensation come from?

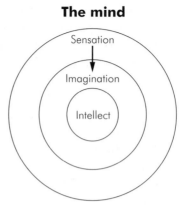

The mind

The existence of material things and their nature

> **Read** *Meditation 6* paragraphs 5–21, particularly 19–21

If the imagination finds its origin in sensation, then this leaves Descartes with a new question: where do our sensations come from? Descartes' attempt to answer this question heralds his proof for the existence of material things. The argument is quite complex, so it will be helpful if we divide it into three separate steps.

Step 1: Sensations come from outside of me

Other than those (clear and distinct) features which are the subject matter of mathematics and geometry (shape, position, size, number), there are other (obscure and confused) qualities of objects which are the principal subject matter of imagination. These qualities (colours, smells, etc.) appear to originate in sensation. Descartes recalls his initial (pre-doubt) view of sensory ideas and their origin. On this view all his ideas, both the clear and distinct, and the obscure and confused, are caused in him by the existence of material things outside of his mind. Physical objects were thought to be the source of these ideas, and they projected representations of themselves into his mind. Can he now prove that this was basically a correct view? What in it is true and what misleading?

To answer these questions he points to two features of his sensations which suggest they do not emanate from his essential nature as a thinking thing. For if he can show that they do not come from within, it must follow that they must come from somewhere else. The first feature he points to is the fact that they are not subject to his *will*. That is to say, he is unable to control their appearance (after all, you cannot look at this page and choose to see the ink as red). He cannot see or hear whatever he pleases. But since his will is part of his essence as a thinking thing, this suggests that they are not produced from within him, but by some *other* power.

Secondly he observes that his sensations are (in a sense) *extended*. That is, they appear to represent things which have size and shape. But he himself (i.e. his mind) is unextended. It has no size or shape and cannot be divided into pieces, since different faculties of the mind (the will, imagination, etc.) are not different parts of him, but are all aspects of the same mind. So although sensations occur within his mind, in the sense that they are aspects or 'modes' of his consciousness, they do not and cannot arise spontaneously within such a mind. For mind is non-spatial and whatever is non-spatial, Descartes maintains, cannot create something which is spatial. So again sensations must come from outside of him.

Step 2: Sensations originate in matter

So where could sensations come from? Two possibilities suggest themselves. They could come from the material world, where I had always thought they came from, or they could come from God (pp. 157–8). However, I have a strong natural inclination to believe that there is a physical world and I have no faculty or means by which to discover that this is not so. Now, as we have seen, I can only be deceived if I allow myself to be. So if there is a belief that I have no means of correcting, then God would not allow me to be deceived about it, and therefore my sensations must originate in material objects, just as they appear to. And these must contain those properties which I clearly and distinctly perceive.

Step 3: Primary and secondary qualities

The next question concerns what the material world is actually like. It certainly isn't quite like it appears to be, as has been established by the arguments from illusion of *Meditation 1*. Descartes' answer is that only some of the perceived features of objects are actually in them, while the remainder are mere effects made upon the mind by these objects. In other words he draws a distinction between the primary or real qualities of objects and the secondary or merely apparent ones. The way he draws the distinction is to claim that he can be certain that those features he clearly and distinctly perceives to be in objects must really be in objects since God would not allow him to be deceived about what he clearly and distinctly perceives. So those features of his sensations, those that are amenable to mathematical and geometric description, must be the real qualities of objects. However, those qualities which he perceives only obscurely and confusedly, such as colour, smell, heat and so on, and which do not lend themselves to mathematical description, cannot be relied upon to make judgements about. And so we should not jump to the supposition that they exist in objects.

Descartes subscribes to the theory of perception known as REPRESENTATIVE REALISM. According to this theory, 'ideas' or sensations are private representations of physical things. These things have primary qualities such as extension, mass, motion and quantity (the subject matter of mathematics and geometry). Such qualities are inherent features of matter itself. In addition to primary qualities there are secondary qualities such as sounds, smells, colours, tastes and textures which are simply the way matter appears to a perceiving mind. These secondary qualities are not directly representative. Thus matter itself is not coloured, rather there are powers or dispositions in matter which cause us to perceive colours.

■ **Figure 9.2**
Primary and secondary qualities
According to representative realism, some aspects of our sensations are accurate while others are not. So our representation of the so-called primary qualities of size, shape, position and motion represent accurately what is out there. Physical objects really have these properties. But our experiences of colour, sound, smell, taste and so on do not. These properties do not exist in themselves in the same way that primary qualities do. Rather such sensations are imperfect representations produced by the secondary qualities of objects. So our different experiences of smells represent different shapes of molecules, for example.

Perceived object

Real object

Summary of the main steps to establish the existence of matter in *Meditation 6*

Descartes introduces the proof of the existence of matter with a discussion of the distinction between imagination and intellect. The imagination is not a part of his essence, so where does it come from? Descartes conjectures that it consists in the mind 'turning' its attention to material bodies, and that its origin lies in sensation. So where do sensations come from?

STEP 1 Descartes argues that sensations must have their origin in material, extended bodies. To this end he produces two parallel arguments leading to the same conclusion.

a)

Premise 1 The will is a part of my essence.

Premise 2 Sensation is not subject to my will.

Conclusion Sensations come from outside of me.

b)

Premise 1 My nature or essence is unextended.

Premise 2 Sensations are ideas of extended things.

Conclusion Sensations come from outside of me.

STEP 2 Having established that sensations come from outside of him, Descartes now attempts to prove that their origin is in material bodies.

Premise 1 There are two possible sources for the origin of sensation: God or matter.

Premise 2 I have a strong natural inclination to believe they come from matter, and I have no faculty by which to correct this belief.

Intermediate

conclusion So if their origin were in God, God would be a deceiver.

Premise 3 God is not a deceiver.

Conclusion Sensation originates in matter.

STEP 3 Descartes now knows that the material world exists. But what exactly is it like?

Premise 1 God would not allow me to be deceived in judgements based on clear and distinct ideas.

Premise 2 I have a clear and distinct idea of the geometric and mathematical properties I perceive in matter.

Conclusion Therefore I can correctly judge that material objects really possess mathematical and geometric properties.

Interpretation and evaluation

Now that you are familiar with the way Descartes proves the existence of the material world we need to consider objections.

■ Problems with Step 1 of the argument

Descartes claims that sensations cannot come from within him since: a) they are not subject to his will; b) they are representations of extended things, while he is an unextended thinking thing.

Dreams are not subject to my will

▶ criticism ◀ We may note that dreams are not subject to our will any more than our sensations are, and yet they certainly come from within us. This shows that not everything that is not subject to my will must come from outside of the mind. So perhaps sensations come from a part of me of which I am not conscious.

Why couldn't an extended thing create extended ideas?

▶ criticism ◀ Secondly, we could argue that it is not clearly and distinctly obvious that an unextended thing could never produce the idea of an extended thing. Descartes' thought involves appeal, once again, to his causal principle, claiming that we cannot produce something from nothing and so cannot get extension out of an unextended thing. But if there is a real problem here, we might wonder how it is possible for an unextended thing to have perceptions of extended things at all. If the mind is truly unextended, then in what sense can its perceptions be extended? And if we are able to perceive representations of extended things although we are unextended, why not be able to dream them up too?

■ Problems with Step 2 of the argument

▶ criticism ◀ If we accept the conclusion that sensations originate outside of us, must we follow Descartes in Step 2 of the argument that they cannot come from a non-deceiving God, and so must come from matter?

Couldn't God be the origin of sensation?

▶ criticism ◀ Perhaps God feeds the ideas of material things directly into our minds. This is a view held by the empiricist philosopher George Berkeley (1685–1753).[31] This might be thought a far more efficient way of arranging things since it produces the same effect without having to bother with a material world. Descartes rejects this possibility on the grounds that it would be a grave deception on God's part to make us think there is a material world when there isn't. However, can we really know what would be for the best in such matters? It might be a deception, but one that is in our best interests, and Descartes doesn't seem to be in any position to be able to determine the matter. In any case, would this really be a deception? Berkeley certainly didn't believe so. He argued that the very idea of a material world, in the sense of something lying beyond our perception, is a philosophical confusion. We cannot make coherent sense of this idea of 'matter' since it is the idea of a thing of which we could never have any experience. What we perceive are our own sensations or 'ideas', and what we mean by a material object is nothing more than a collection of such sensations. It is the supposition that there is something more, something lying beyond the sensations of which I am directly aware in my mind, that is the error.

We are already deceived about secondary qualities, so why not primary?

▶ criticism ◀ The thought that God might have arranged things so that we are indeed deceived about the nature of what causes our experiences is given added credence when we consider that we already know that we are deceived about the independent existence of *secondary* qualities. We tend to believe objects really possess colours, smells, tastes and so on and yet, according to Descartes, this is an error. But this is an error into which we naturally seem to fall, and so surely God might also allow us to be deceived about the independent existence of the *primary* qualities. Moreover, we also know, as Descartes points out in *Meditation 1*, that our senses are often deceptive. Doesn't this show that God is a deceiver anyway? And if he deceives us, how can we possibly rely on him to ensure our senses are reliable about anything?

David Hume makes this criticism of Descartes in his *Enquiry Concerning Human Understanding*:

> To have recourse to the veracity of the Supreme Being, in order to prove the veracity of our senses, is surely making a very unexpected circuit. If his veracity were at all concerned in this matter, our senses would be entirely infallible; because it is not possible that he can ever deceive.
>
> Section 12, part 1, p. 202

What he is saying here is that using God to guarantee the trustworthiness of the senses as evidence for the existence of the world cannot work, because if God were at all involved here he would not allow us to be deceived at all. The fact that we are so often deceived shows he cannot be involved in guaranteeing the reliability of our senses.

Descartes' response to these points would be to accept that we have a natural inclination to believe that objects actually possess colours as real qualities. However, the key point is that in this case God has allowed us to escape from this deception by the use of our reason, which is to say, by relying on clear and distinct ideas. And similarly with illusions and sense deception: in these cases we are able to detect the error. However, by contrast, we have no means of correcting the belief that bodies have sizes, shapes, positions and motions. We have no way of discovering that the whole physical universe is a grand illusion. So if the primary qualities were not real, or the physical world didn't exist at all, we would be subject to an *inescapable* deception, and it is this that he regards as incompatible with God's power and goodness.

We cannot penetrate the veil of perception

▶ criticism ◀ It has often been urged as a criticism of representative realism that, if we only have access to the sensations *within* our own minds, there can be no absolute guarantee that anything beyond our own minds exists. Berkeley's arguments are once again instructive here. We can only ever observe our own perceptions and so we are caught behind a 'veil of perception'. If all we can truly know about is what enters into our own experience and we can never experience material reality directly, then we can have no ultimate proof that it exists. Descartes' approach, it can be argued, leads us into solipsism.[32]

God may not exist anyway

▶ criticism ◀ Even if we accept that an all-powerful, all-good God wouldn't deceive us about the existence of the material world, this simply throws us back onto the question of the success of Descartes' proofs for God's existence. If we have good reason to suppose that these do not succeed, which we have argued above that we do, then there is no guarantee that we are not being radically deceived, and so the world may be very different from the way it appears, or worse, it may not exist. Descartes' reliance on God to escape scepticism means that any failure to prove his existence has a heavy price: solipsism.

■ Problems with Step 3 of the argument

Matter might not be essentially geometric

▶ criticism ◀ If we grant the existence of matter, must we accept that it is in essence pure extension, as Descartes claims in Step 3? In other words, must we accept the primary/secondary quality distinction? Even if we admit that the geometric properties of physical things can be reasoned about in an *a priori* manner and can be 'clearly and distinctly' understood, we need not conclude from this that such properties are really out there. It is one thing to say that geometry is *a priori*, and another to say that matter is in essence purely geometric. Some philosophers, such as Kant, have argued that the world as it is in itself may be radically different from the way it appears and may not include spatio-temporal dimensions. Kant argued that we cannot say anything about the world as it is in itself since it lies behind the 'veil of perception', and that geometry is a description of the way the world *appears* to us, rather than how it really is.

Matter has causal properties

► CRITICISM ◄ We may also argue that there is more to matter than pure extension in space; for example, matter has 'mass' as described by Newton some thirty years later than the *Meditations*, which accounts for the manner in which an object moves through space, what happens when it collides with another object, and so on. In other words, there is more to a physical object than just position, number, motion and extension; it also possesses various causal properties which are to do with the material substance of which it is composed. Our idea of matter includes as an essential component the notion that it is made of some sort of brute *stuff*, and is not just empty space. It is the fact that different kinds of material object are made of different kinds of stuff that accounts for the fact that different things act and react in different ways.

The distinction between mind and body

The view that the mind and the body are distinct substances is known as *substance* DUALISM, or *Cartesian dualism* after Descartes himself. Descartes puts forward two principal arguments to establish this distinction in the *Meditations*. Here we will outline two.

First argument for the real distinction: the epistemological argument

Read *Meditation 6* paragraphs 16 and 17

If I can (clearly and distinctly) distinguish the essences of two things they must be distinguishable in principle. In other words, if they have different natures they must be two substances even though they are mixed together. Descartes makes this point by saying that if I can *think* of two things separately it is possible in principle, or, if you like, *logically* possible, for them to be separated. And if it is possible to separate them then they could be separated by God.

Descartes then repeats his claim from *Meditation 2*, where, you may recall, he argued that the only thing he was aware of being a part of his essence was thinking and concludes that his essence must be thinking. This time, however, he wants to make the stronger claim that because this conception of his essence is clear and distinct he can now know that he is *nothing more* than a thinking thing.

... from the mere fact that I know with certainty that I exist, and that I do not observe that any other thing belongs necessarily to my nature or essence except that I am a thinking thing, I rightly conclude that my essence consists in this alone, that I am a thinking thing, or a substance whose whole essence of nature consists in thinking. (p. 156)

I also have a clear and distinct conception of my body, namely that it is in essence an extended thing. But this conception of body is *not* essential to the idea of myself, and therefore it is certain that I am really distinct from my body and can exist apart from it. In other words the mind and the body are distinct *substances*. It is worth emphasising here that Descartes thinks he has established that mind and body are distinct *substances* since a substance is definable as something which can exist separated from anything else.

Part of Descartes' idea is just to point out that what we mean when we talk about minds is something radically unlike what we mean when talking about bodies. They are completely different sorts of thing. Bodies can get wet, or hot, but minds cannot. And minds can get angry or pensive and bodies cannot. Bodies are 'machines' subject to deterministic natural laws. Minds are reasoning thinking agents. Bodies are necessarily extended in space, but my mind, with its thoughts and ideas, cannot be thought of as having size or shape.

We can summarise Descartes' argument like this:

Premise 1 I clearly and distinctly perceive myself (i.e. my mind) to be only a thinking and unextended thing.

Premise 2 I clearly and distinctly perceive my body to be only an extended and unthinking thing.

Conclusion My mind is not my body.

Interpretation and evaluation

▶ criticism ◀ The argument outlined above rests heavily on the supposition that Descartes can perceive the essential natures of both mind and body by thought alone. Descartes believes that, when contemplating his mind and his idea of body, he has a clear and distinct grasp of both and it is only because he truly perceives the essential differences that he can conclude with confidence that they really are different. But, as we saw when examining his discussion of his knowledge of himself in *Meditation 2*, Descartes' efforts to divine an object's essential nature are based purely on what one can and cannot conceive, in other words on what we called the 'subjective' approach to discovering essences. But this is not a reliable method. There could yet be aspects to himself which he is not directly aware of. In other words, his essence may not be thought *alone*. Thought might still be the product of some material processes in his brain of which he is not aware, as we saw Gassendi argue on page 56 of this book. Perhaps in perceiving the mind and body as separate he is merely perceiving two different aspects of the same thing. So just because there *appear* to be two things here would not necessarily mean that there really *are* two things.

To see the flaw, consider a parallel argument. I have a clear and distinct perception of heat. My idea here is simple, readily recognisable and I don't perceive anything else to be part of this idea. I also have a clear and distinct idea of motion. Again I can recognise movement and appear to understand everything which is a part of this idea. Yet, can I conclude from this that heat and motion are totally different? Certainly they appear very different and so, from the subjective point of view, I would have to say that they have different essences. And yet, if science is to be believed, heat turns out to be no more or less than the vibration of molecules and atoms. Heat, in other words, is reducible to motion: despite appearances, they are not in reality different. So even though two ideas can be conceived of separately, it does not follow that they must be separate in reality. Descartes' error is to suppose that by contemplating the natures of mind and body he is determining their objective essences, whereas he is really only describing the way they appear to him.

The masked-man fallacy

more difficult

In trying to distinguish objects on the basis of what can or cannot be conceived, Descartes may be accused of committing what is often termed the *masked-man fallacy*. To understand this fallacy we need to begin by clarifying a key move in Descartes' argument. In arguing for the distinction of body and mind Descartes is making implicit use of a principle that later became known as Leibniz's law. Leibniz's law states that if two things are in fact the same, then everything which is true of the one must also be true of the other. But if there is anything which is true of one, which is *not* true of the other, then they must be different things.

Although it sounds complex, the principle is intuitively easy to grasp. Consider the following examples: At the time of writing, 'Tony Blair' and 'the present Prime Minister' are different names for the same person. So anything that is true of Tony Blair will also be true of the present Prime Minister and vice versa. For example, if it is true that Tony Blair is married to Cherie, then it must also be true that the present Prime Minister is married to Cherie. And if it is true that the present Prime Minister is 50, then it must also be true that Tony Blair is 50. At the same time everything that is false about Tony Blair will also be false about the present Prime Minister. So, for example, if it is false that Tony Blair smokes a pipe, then it is also false that the present Prime Minister smokes a pipe.

Note that it is very hard to prove that two things are in fact the same using this law, as many things will be true of very different people. For example, it is true of both Tony Blair and George W. Bush that they are politicians, who speak English, wear suits, and have full heads of hair, but this doesn't mean they are the same person. To prove that two things really are the same using this method we would need to enumerate *all* their qualities. But to prove that two things are different is much easier: all we need to do is to find just one thing that is true of the one which is not true of the other. So, the fact that George W. Bush is not the Prime Minister shows that he is not Tony Blair.

This same principle is used in courts of law every day. Imagine a murder case in which the accused is called Finbar Good. The prosecution are trying to prove that 'the murderer' and 'Finbar Good' refer to the same person. They do this by showing that lots of things that are true of the murderer are also true of Finbar Good. For example:

The murderer was left-handed.
Finbar Good is left-handed.
The murderer was in Peckham on Friday the 13th.
Finbar Good was in Peckham on Friday the 13th.

This could even go right down to:

The murderer has fingerprint xyz.
Finbar Good has fingerprint xyz.

The defence, however, are trying to show that Finbar Good and the murderer are not the same person, by trying to prove that what is true of the murderer is not true of Finbar Good. For example:

The murderer was over 6 feet tall
Finbar Good is 5 feet 6 inches tall.

If these last two claims are both true, then it follows that Finbar cannot be the murderer. So this application of Leibniz's law is clearly valid.

Descartes' argument for the difference between body and mind follows similar lines. Descartes is trying to show that his mind is distinct from his body, in other words, that they are separate entities. And in order to do this, all he needs to do is show that something is true of his mind that is not true of his body. Hence he writes:

... because on the one hand, I have a clear and distinct idea of myself in so far as I am a thinking and unextended thing, and because, on the other hand I have a distinct idea of the body in so far as it is an unextended thing but which does not think, it is certain that I, that is to say my mind ... is entirely and truly distinct from my body. (p. 156)

In the passage Descartes puts forward two differences between his self or mind, and his body; namely that he is aware of one as being conscious and unextended, and the other as being extended but not conscious. So we can distinguish two separate arguments:

Premise 1 I have an idea of my mind as a thinking thing.
Premise 2 I have an idea of my body as a non-thinking thing.

Conclusion Therefore my mind and body are different.

Premise 1 I have an idea of my body as an extended thing.
Premise 2 I have an idea of myself as an unextended thing.

Conclusion Therefore my mind and body are different.

By applying Leibniz's law here it seems Descartes can prove that the mind and the body are distinct entities and that they do not depend on each other for their existence. However, there is an important exception to Leibniz's law. In 'intentional' contexts, it does not hold. Intentional contexts are those that involve the mind's thinking *about* or being aware *of* something, such as when it has a belief, a hope, or a desire. Beliefs, hopes and desires are said to be intentional states, in that they are directed at something in the world, or are about something. Now, since here Descartes' argument involves the intentional states of being aware of his body and mind, and having an idea of their properties, he cannot apply Leibniz's law. This is because Descartes' awareness of his body and mind need not reveal the true nature of either. In other words, while Descartes may have an *idea* of his body as extended and unthinking, and an *idea* of his mind as unextended and thinking, this doesn't guarantee that the two really do possess these properties in themselves.

To understand the point, consider the following argument.

Premise 1 My idea of Batman is of a masked crusader.
Premise 2 My idea of Bruce Wayne is not of a masked crusader.

Conclusion Therefore Batman is not Bruce Wayne.

This argument is clearly fallacious since Bruce Wayne could well be Batman if, on occasion and unbeknown to me, he dresses up in a cape and mask to perform heroic deeds. And in the same way, my mind could well be my body if, unbeknown to me, the activities of some part of it, say my brain, are able to produce conscious experiences. The fact that I am unaware of my brain doing this doesn't show that it doesn't, so while my mind and body may appear very different, in reality they could still be the same.

Note, however, that we may have distorted Descartes' arguments somewhat in making this criticism. While he does state the argument in intentional terms, he is careful to say 'I have a *clear and distinct idea* of myself in so far as I am a thinking and unextended thing, and ... a *distinct idea* of the body in so far as it is an unextended thing but which does not think' (our emphases). The fact that his awareness of his body and mind are said to be 'clear and distinct' clearly involves for Descartes the claim that his awareness reveals the true nature of each. After all, he has been arguing that whatever he clearly and distinctly perceives must be true and so he is not simply distinguishing the way mind and body appear to him, but rather talking about their real properties. So perhaps a fairer interpretation of his arguments would be:

Premise 1 The true nature of my mind is a thinking thing.
Premise 2 The true nature of my body is a non-thinking thing.

Conclusion Therefore my mind and body are different.

Premise 1 The true nature of my body is an extended thing.
Premise 2 The true nature of my mind is an unextended thing.

Conclusion Therefore my mind and body are different.

In this version the criticism above does not hold, as the key differences identified are not intentional states but real properties of the objects in question. So if the premises of these arguments are true we must accept the conclusion. However the problem now is whether we should accept these premises. In other words, can we be sure that Descartes' ideas of his mind and body are accurate? For while it may well be true that Descartes believes himself to have a clear and distinct idea of himself as an unextended thing, this is not quite the same thing as saying he really *is* an unextended thing. Materialist philosophers, those who believe that the mind is in fact a physical phenomenon of some sort, will deny the second premises of both arguments and claim that the mind is indeed extended (for example, they may claim it occupies the same space as the brain) and that the body is indeed capable of thought (for example, consciousness may be produced by the electrochemical activity of the brain).

So does Descartes really have a clear and distinct idea of his mind as unextended and of his body as non-thinking?

One reason to think not is that it is difficult to see how he could ever be clearly and distinctly aware that his mind and body *lack* any property at all. While he may not be aware of his body being able to think or of his mind being extended this is not the same as being able positively to say that they couldn't be. In other words, it is not that he is aware that his body and mind lack these qualities, rather it is that he is not aware that they have them. All that Descartes can clearly and distinctly know is that when he examines his idea of his body, he is unaware of its being able to think, and when he examines his mind he is unaware of its being extended. So his arguments should really be of the following form:

Premise 1 I am aware of myself as a thinking thing.
Premise 2 I am not aware of my body as a thinking thing.

Conclusion Therefore my mind and body are different.

Premise 1 I am aware of my body as an extended thing.
Premise 2 I am not aware of myself as an extended thing.

Conclusion Therefore my mind and body are different.

However, these arguments are again guilty of committing the masked-man fallacy as they involve intentional contexts. Just because he is not aware of his mind and body in either of these ways is not the same as saying that they cannot be such. To see this point again, consider the following example. Imagine you are at a masked ball, in which the identity of all the guests is disguised. Someone enters the room wearing an elaborate mask and you try to reason as to the identity of this person along the following lines:

Premise 1   I am aware that my best friend has a scar on his cheek.

Premise 2   I am not aware that the man in the mask has a scar on his cheek.

Conclusion   Therefore the man in the mask is not my best friend.

Here something is true of your friend – that you are aware he has a scar on his cheek – that is not true of the man in the mask. Both premises are true, and so it would seem that, according to Leibniz's law, the two terms 'best friend' and 'man in the mask' cannot refer to the same person. There must be two people involved. However this is plainly wrong. The man in the mask could be your best friend, but with a mask on. Leibniz's law fails in this instance because the two premises of the argument tell us more about your state of mind than about the man's scarring. So the fact that you are unaware of his scar doesn't tell us anything for sure about whether or not he actually has a scar in reality. In other words, not being aware that he has a scar, is not the same as being aware that he doesn't have a scar, yet it is this premise that is needed for Leibniz's law to apply.

In the same way imagine if someone, Kevin, did not follow politics very closely and doesn't know who the Prime Minster is at the moment. After asking Kevin several questions we might be able to put the following argument together.

Premise 1   Kevin is aware that the Prime Minister works in the Houses of Parliament.

Premise 2   Kevin is not aware that Tony Blair works in the Houses of Parliament.

Conclusion   Therefore Tony Blair is not the Prime Minister.

Again the conclusion is plainly false, even though the premises may be true since they reveal no real differences in the objects themselves (the Prime Minister and Tony Blair), but merely in the way he is conceived by Kevin. Not knowing that Tony Blair works in the Houses of Parliament, is not the same as knowing that he doesn't, and this is what would be needed for Leibniz's law to work here; likewise with Descartes' argument. Not being aware that his mind is extended is not the same as being aware that it is not. And not being aware of his body as a thinking thing is not the same as being aware that it is not. Putting forward differences between the mind and body on the basis of what he is or is not aware of does not really tell us that minds and bodies are in fact different. Minds may well be extended. And bodies may well be thinking.

ACTIVITY   Why do these arguments commit the masked-man fallacy?

1 Premise 1 The president believes that Eminem has destroyed the moral fibre of the country.

Premise 2 The president does not believe that Marshall Mathers has destroyed the moral fibre of the country.

Conclusion Therefore Eminem is not Marshall Mathers.

2 Premise 1 Derren knows that the morning star is the planet Venus.

Premise 2 Derren does not know that the evening star is the planet Venus.

Conclusion Therefore the morning star is not the evening star.

3 Premise 1 Abi wants to become famous.

Premise 2 Abi does not want to be hounded by the press and general public.

Conclusion Therefore becoming famous does not involve being hounded by the press and general public.

4 Premise 1 Britney wants to marry William.

Premise 2 Britney does not want to marry the heir to the throne.

Conclusion Therefore William is not the heir to the throne.

5 Premise 1 I am aware of looking out for my own safety when crossing roads.

Premise 2 I am not aware of having a guardian angel who looks out for my safety when crossing roads.

Conclusion Therefore my safety depends only on myself and not on a guardian angel.

Second argument: the argument from divisibility

Read Meditation 6 paragraph 17

When I look into myself I find 'one single and complete thing' (p. 164). And whether my mind is concerned with experiencing a pain in the foot, seeing a goat, imagining a sunny day, or considering a philosophical problem it is all the time the same self or mind which is enjoying these conscious experiences. For aspects of thought, such as willing, understanding, imagining or perceiving, are not parts that could be removed from me since it is the same mind that wills, understands, perceives or imagines. In other words, my self is unitary and indivisible. I am a single centre of consciousness and my consciousness cannot be divided into parts.

Contrast this now with the body. Any physical thing, in virtue of being extended, can always be divided up into parts, at least in principle. Since mind and body differ in this important way, they must be different substances.

Premise 1 My mind is indivisible.
Premise 2 My body is divisible.

Conclusion My mind is not my body.

Interpretation and evaluation

Descartes initially puts forward the argument in a non-intentional context.

... there is a great difference between mind and body, in that body, by its nature, is always divisible and that mind is entirely indivisible. (p. 164)

We will return to this below.

However, the subsequent passage also contains an intentional version of the argument:

... when I consider the mind ... I can distinguish no parts ... But it is quite the opposite in corporeal or extended things, for there is none that I cannot easily take to pieces in thought. (p. 164)

In this latter case, the argument amounts more or less to the following:

Premise 1 I cannot conceive of my mind as being divisible.
Premise 2 I can only conceive of physical things as being divisible.

Conclusion My mind is not a physical thing.

▶ criticism ◀ In this version, the premises may well be true, however the argument involves an intentional context and, as such, constitutes the exception to Leibniz's law, making it invalid. In other words, this is another example of the masked-man fallacy. Just because his mind appears to Descartes to be indivisible, doesn't mean it really is. In this case the premises are true but the conclusion does not follow.

However, the initial formulation which makes claims about the real essence of mind and body, independently of the way it appears to his mind, was presented as follows.

Premise 1 My mind is indivisible.
Premise 2 My body is divisible.

Conclusion My mind is not my body.

Because it is not framed in an intentional context, this is clearly valid and, as such, if the premises are true the conclusion would follow. So the question here is to determine whether it is true that the mind is indivisible and the body divisible.

There does seem to be something important about the nature of consciousness that Descartes has hit upon in this argument. Our minds do seem to have a unified nature. I am a single conscious entity and all my conscious experiences necessarily belong to the one thing that I am. So while we know from neuroscience that our brains are composed of millions of individual cells and that our brains, like all physical objects, are divisible, we do not experience the mind as a combination of billions of individual events, but as an indivisible, singular consciousness. Surely this must mean that the mind cannot be the brain.

▶ criticism ◀ However, the sense that I am a unitary centre of consciousness could be an illusion. As we have seen, what we perceive when we look into our own minds may not be the true nature of ourselves. If consciousness is indeed a product of the brain, then cutting up the brain might well literally involve dividing the self, and this view gets support from neurological evidence. Operations which involve severing the connection between the left and right hemispheres of the brain seem to divide consciousness. People who have had this operation will display behaviours which suggest a divided consciousness, with the left hand literally not knowing what the right hand is doing. Observations of monkeys with split brains appear to show them getting hold of a peanut with both hands and having a tug of war with themselves.[33]

▶ criticism ◀ We saw earlier that Hume argues that the concept of 'self' does not involve a singular thing which has my experiences. When we look into our minds, we do not discover, he argues, any such unitary self, all we are ever aware of is a series of conscious experiences, never anything which is having these experiences. If Hume is right, then Descartes is misdescribing the way his mind appears to himself. He has no immediate consciousness of an indivisible self. I am aware of experiences, but I am nothing over and above these experiences. Since there is no reason to think my experiences might not be separated one from another, it is not true to say that I cannot be divided.

Having established the existence of material things and the real distinction between mind and body, the rest of the *Meditation* is taken up with Descartes' explanation of the relationship between the mind and the body and his account of the true nature of the material world.

The relation of mind and body

Read *Meditation 6* paragraphs 22–end

We have begun to see the characteristic distinctions that Descartes draws between mind and body. Firstly the mind is *thought*, the body *extension*. So while the body is in essence something which is extended in three-dimensional space, the mind is unextended: it has no size or shape. Part of Descartes' idea here is that it is meaningless to talk about the mind or mental states as possessing extended properties. For example, it makes no sense to say that my mind is triangular or round, large or small. The belief that goats eat grass cannot be oval or square; the desire for coffee cannot be three inches long. To speak about the self or mental states in these terms is to talk nonsense.

Secondly the body is *divisible* and the mind *indivisible*. If I take a sturdy axe it is perfectly possible to cleave someone's body in two, and then into four, eight, and so on indefinitely. However, I can never do this with their mind. The very idea of dividing one's self is inconceivable. I am one centre of consciousness and could never be divided from myself. Removing someone's limbs, while it would involve separating parts of their body from them, would not involve separating parts of their *self*. You cannot remove bits of the self, as you can remove bits of the body. It would still be the same person, without legs, arms or even a torso.

Also, the mind is *private* but bodies are publicly observable. Anyone can (at least in principle) inspect any aspect of my physical body; but I have a privileged view of my mind: only I directly know what I am thinking and feeling. I can entertain a thought and keep it to myself, and no one else will be able to tell what it is, unless I decide to tell them. Moreover, because I look immediately into my mind, I can form indubitable beliefs about my states of consciousness. That is, I cannot be mistaken about what I am thinking or feeling; I have infallible access to my private mental realm. So if I am daydreaming about my summer holidays or suffering a headache, for example, I *know* that I am. I cannot believe I am when in reality I am not. It would be absurd for someone to claim to be unsure of what they were thinking or feeling. By contrast, when it comes to making judgements about what is going on in my body, or in other physical bodies, I can make mistakes. The senses can deceive me as when a square tower in the distance appears round (p. 154). Certain disorders such as dropsy can cause thirst when the body doesn't need water (p. 163), and amputees still appear to have sensations in their missing limb (p. 167).

Finally, the mind is free to follow its own train of thought. So I can plan my holidays and there are no constraints on where I can imagine going or what I can imagine doing. Or, if I prefer, I could meditate on a philosophical problem and jump to a rash conclusion. In other words, I have free will, which allows me to think what I choose. But material bodies are bound by physical laws and determined in what they do. The physical universe is ultimately just a great machine; each of its parts following blindly the path it is determined to tread by the ineluctable laws of nature. While I can fly in my imagination – that is to say, in my *mind* – if my body falls out of the window, no amount of arm flapping will prevent the law of gravity propelling it toward its demise.

Summary of the main distinctions between mind and body according to Descartes

Mind	Body
Unextended	**Extended**
The essence of mind is pure consciousness or thought. The intellect which performs the *cogito* constitutes my essence.	The essence of body is three-dimensionality. It possesses the primary qualities of extension, motion, position and number. Material things cannot use reason and cannot be conscious.
The mind also possesses the inessential properties, or modes, of sensation and imagination, which are the product of its union with the material body.	The secondary qualities of colour, sound, smell, etc. do not really exist in objects, but are projections of perceiving minds.
Indivisible	**Divisible**
The mind or self is one. It cannot be divided into parts. You cannot be half a mind or self.	All physical things can be divided into smaller pieces, at least in principle.
Neither can mental states such as beliefs, sensations, etc. be divided into parts.	There are no atoms and no vacuums. That is, there are no indivisible units, and no empty spaces.

Continued

Private	Public
I enjoy privileged access to the contents of my own mind. Other minds cannot look into my mind.	All physical things are open to public view.
Known directly	**Known indirectly**
I perceive the contents of my own mind, including my own sensations, directly or immediately.	I perceive physical things only indirectly, via my sensations. Sensations are representations of material things, a view known as representative realism.
Indubitable	**Dubitable**
I cannot doubt the existence of my mind; nor can I be mistaken about what I am conscious of. I have infallible access to my mental states. (The *cogito* argument)	I can doubt the existence of material things, including the existence of my own body. (The Evil Demon Argument)
Free	**Determined**
Minds are free to think what they please. They can follow a train of thought and are free to choose what to do.	Physical bodies are bound by natural laws. They cannot choose how to behave.
Creative	**Predetermined**
Minds can create new ideas, understand and form sentences never uttered before, and act in new and original ways. They can use language and understand mathematics.	Physical things cannot create new ideas, understand new sentences or react in new ways to their environments. They cannot use language or understand mathematics.

But despite these differences the mind and body do come into a relationship of causal interaction. What this means is that the mind can cause things to happen in the body and the body in the mind, as is evidenced by our everyday experience. For example, I can will my arm to move to scratch my nose, and this act of will occurring in my mind causes my body to move. My desire to see a particular film, coupled with my belief that it is showing at the local cinema – both mental states or events – cause my body to don my coat, leave the house and walk to the cinema, and so on.

The process leading to my arm moving begins in the mind and enters the body in the brain, and Descartes conjectures that the causal connection occurs in a small gland which he calls the 'common sense', today known as the pineal gland (p. 165). From here, the process can be traced through the brain, down the spinal column and along the arm via the nerves. The way Descartes views this process is partly figured by his understanding of hydraulics, and he supposes that a very fine liquid or 'spirit' operating under pressure pushes along the nerves to produce the action in the arm. This substance is what *animates* the body and hence is known as 'animal spirits'.

Causal interaction also works in the other direction, so that physical events in my body can cause events in my mind. For example, if I damage my foot by stepping on a nail, the animal spirits transmit the sensory information to my brain. It is then channelled to the pineal gland and passes over into the mind which experiences the pain. Notice that even though the message arrives in the mind and causes it to have the sensation, the pain is nonetheless experienced as though it were in the foot. So the mind is able to project sensations out into the body. Significantly, the system is not foolproof and it is possible for the information arriving at the brain to be misleading. Descartes likens the nerves leading from my foot to my brain to a series of stretched cords tied together: if you pull at the foot end, the movement will be communicated from one cord to another along the entire length and a tug will be felt in the brain. But if I pull at the knee cord, half-way along the series, the movement arriving at the brain end will be indistinguishable from one that had originated in the foot. In this way, Descartes explains phantom limb syndrome, the tendency of those who have lost limbs to continue to experience pains where their limbs once were (p. 165).

■ **Figure 9.3**

The mind is in causal interaction with the body via the pineal gland, or 'common sense' in the centre of the brain. Its relationship with the extended body is mediated by 'animal spirits' which transmit information along the nerves.

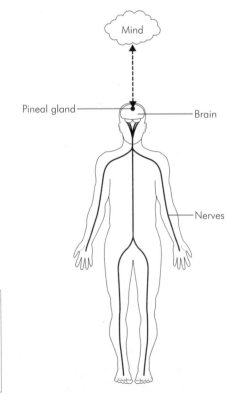

NB Descartes does not actually use the term 'pineal gland' in The Meditations but in a letter to Mersenne in 1641 (same year as The Meditations published) he refers to the 'common sense' being the pineal gland.

And it is the same process which accounts for all perceptions. The sensation of thirst, a mental occurrence, is (normally) caused by dehydration of the body and is communicated to the mind via the nerves; and so too with our sensations of objects beyond our own bodies. I will be caused to see a goat when light bouncing off the goat enters my eye and affects my retina in various ways, which in turn causes changes to occur within my brain. Finally, the causal chain of events leading from the goat to my brain passes over into the mind and I have a sense-experience of a goat.

So, in summary, Descartes is telling us that unextended mind comes into causal contact with the body somewhere in the centre of the brain where it picks up signals from the body, and from other physical things, and in turn manoeuvres the body around within the world. This account may remind us of a driver steering a vehicle, as though my self or mind were somehow lodged inside my skull receiving information about my body via a network of nerves and learning about the world via the sense organs. I am able to control this body by freely choosing how to move it through the physical environment. However, this picture is one that Descartes wants to dispel, since in everyday life we do not feel in the least bit detached from our own bodies. I have a special relationship with the body I call mine; one which is very different from my relationship with other physical bodies. I have a peculiar attachment to my body so that when it is damaged it is as though *I* am hurt. Descartes reminds us that 'I am not present in my body merely as a pilot is present in a ship' (p. 159). Rather I am intimately united with my body and feel myself to be at one with it as though my mind were somehow suffused throughout all its parts.

This feeling is natural and no accident. For since God created the world and man's place within it, the lessons of nature cannot be wholly deceitful. In other words if there are beliefs that come naturally to us and are difficult to avoid, then there must be a good reason for our commitment to them. So why, although the mind and body are distinct substances, do we feel intimately intermingled with it? Descartes' answer is that if this were not the case, rather than have the confused experience of pain, I would have the explicit and clear realisation that the body was damaged. Sensations such as pain and thirst are 'confused modes of consciousness' consequent upon the intimate union of mind and body. But clearly it is very useful that we experience pain. For if when I step on a nail I had an explicit understanding of the damage instead of its hurting, I might not react in the appropriate way – I might choose to ignore it and get on with something more interesting rather than clean and bandage the wound. So clearly pain is a very effective message to the mind which elicits the proper responses. Pain, thirst, hunger and so on may not provide a clear and distinct understanding of what is going on in our bodies; but they do give us the proper motivations that allow us to survive. For finite beings like us, it is probably just as well that God has arranged things this way.

As well as making it known that I have a body, nature teaches that my body is surrounded by other bodies. Belief in the material world is, as we have seen, a natural inclination. But nature also appears to teach that these bodies possess qualities such as heat and colour, which has been shown not to be the case. So it would seem that not all the lessons of nature can be trusted. This is also explained by Descartes by reference to the fact that we are not simply thinking things, but are a *compound* of mind and body. The intellect can lead us to certain knowledge of the nature of external objects, since knowledge of the truth is to be discovered by the mind in isolation from the body. But those ideas which are the product of the union of mind and body, namely sensations, are merely indications to the mind of what is good and bad for the composite of mind and body. Thus sensations are, in general, good guides as to the health of the body, but not to the true nature of material reality.

Descartes also reminds us of how our bodily sensations can be deceptive when we are unwell. Just as a clock can break, so too the machine of the body can go wrong and may send the wrong messages to the mind. And, of course, our external senses can also be deceived. But this fact no longer presents Descartes with any serious sceptical concern. For his intellect can draw upon the information gleaned from his other senses and memory to correct these errors (p. 167–8). Even dreams present no further sceptical worries, since his intellect now allows him to recognise an important difference between dreaming and being awake, namely that there is no continuity between one dream and the next. Memory does not connect the events of different dreams together into a single narrative. However, waking life forms a continuous series. When I wake up each morning, I take off where I left off, and it is this continuity which allows me to judge that it is real (p. 168).

Descartes concludes by admitting that human beings remain liable to error because in real life we often have to make judgements and act without having the time to consider the issue carefully.

Summary of the relationship between mind and body according to Descartes

1 They are independent substances. They can exist apart, and will be separated at death.

2 In this life they exist in causal interaction with each other. So, for example, the mind can affect the body when it wills the hand to move to pick up some food; while the body can affect the mind when events in the body, such as low blood sugar levels, cause sensations such as hunger.

3 The body and mind communicate with each other via a small organ in the centre of the brain called the pineal gland. Information is communicated with the parts of the body by means of animal spirits.

4 Although distinct substances, the mind and body are in an intimate union. The mind feels itself projected throughout the body via the animal spirits. So, for example, we feel pains in the body rather than in the mind.

Interpretation and evaluation

■ Descartes gets more empirically minded

It is noteworthy that in *Meditation 6* Descartes shifts emphasis from purely *a priori* reasoning and introduces more empirical evidence of our experience of embodiment in order to flesh out the details of the mind–body relationship. The fact that he has established that the senses are reliable when used in conjunction with the corrective judgement of the intellect means he can now conduct empirical research with some confidence. Hence the increased importance here of the 'lessons of nature' as opposed to confining himself to what the 'light of reason' teaches. While reason has enabled him to describe the outline of the mind–body relationship, it seems that empirical observation will be necessary to figure out precisely how the mechanisms of human physiology work, where exactly the mind and body come into contact and, importantly, what it is actually like to have a body. What this shows is that Descartes' rationalism is intended to provide us only with the foundations for human science. The details of biology, like those of physics, will require a substantial experimental input.

■ The problem of interaction

▶ criticism ◀ Historically, the issue that philosophical followers of Descartes have been most concerned with is how the two substances – the unextended mind and the extended body – are supposed to interact, given that they have such radically different natures. How can a purely spiritual event in my mind – a desire to scratch my nose for example, something occurring totally outside of the physical universe – cause the brute matter of my arm to move? If two things are to interact they need to have something in common, but here there seems to be no common ground. For them to communicate there would need to be some medium in which the transactions might take place, and yet here there can be none. So the very idea of a non-physical mind operating in a physical universe as if it were itself part of a physical process appears to be incoherent.

Consider the problem in this way. The fact that the mind does not exist in space means that it can have no position. But in this case, the idea of its coming into contact with the brain at a particular spot, in the pineal gland or anywhere else, makes no sense. Moreover, how can a substance without extension in space exert force against extended matter? If ordinary matter in space can only be moved by the impact of some other moving object, how is some immaterial thinking substance to influence it? Think here of the impact of two snooker balls: for the one to cause the other to move, they have to come into contact and *touch* each other over an extended part of their two surfaces. But an unextended substance cannot do this.

▶ criticism ◀ Lastly it has been pointed out that Descartes' view seems at odds with well-established physical laws about the conservation of energy and of momentum. The first law of thermodynamics states that, in a closed system, energy cannot be created or destroyed. And the physical universe is thought to be such a system. In other words, in explaining the occurrence of each and every physical event we should not have to refer to any cause outside the physical universe. But if human minds are exerting force on our material bodies, causing them to act in various ways, then the explanation for human behaviour must come from outside of physics. There must be a constant addition of energy into the physical universe as our minds steer our bodies; pushing and pulling them in different directions using a power which is not to be found within matter.

experimenting with ideas

The idea that the mind (or soul) is somehow distinct from the body is a common one; for example, nearly everyone in the world who is religious believes this. However, as we have seen, it is fairly difficult to say how a supposedly non-material thing (our mind) interacts with a material thing (our brain and body), and so how we manage to get anything done at all.

■ **Figure 9.4**
***The problem of
interaction***

*How and where can two
such radically different
substances come into
causal interaction?*

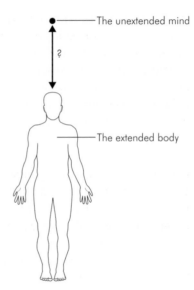

The unextended mind

?

The extended body

Below are some attempted solutions to the problem of interaction.
Look over them and consider the following questions:
1 What problems do you think there are with these solutions?
2 Which of these solutions is closest to your own personal beliefs?
3 Which of these solutions preserves Descartes' distinction between
   the mind and the body?

Solution 1: The mind is in fact the brain. There is no difference
between them. When we talk about mental events (e.g. believing this,
or wanting that) we are just talking about physical (neurological)
events in the brain.

Solution 2: The mind is in fact operating in its own 'immaterial'
world that is exactly parallel to this material world. So, although the
mind and the body do not interact, they do appear to affect each
other. This is a bit like two clocks, clock A, which hasn't got a bell,
and clock B, which has got a bell. When clock A reaches, say,
1 o'clock the bell in clock B sounds, and it appears as if the movement
of the hands in clock A causes the bell to sound in clock B. But these
events are actually causally independent of each other. Similarly, our
minds run parallel to our bodies but are causally independent. So we
feel thirsty (a mental event) and our bodies reach for some water, but
these events have no direct causal relation. So our thirst did not really
cause us to get the water, it just appeared that way.

Solution 3: Our mind and body interact in a special part of our
brain called the 'pineal gland'. This tiny gland at the centre of our
brain allows for the interaction of the immaterial, unextended
substance of our mind with the material, extended substance of our
body.

Solution 4: Our mind is a special type of property that emerges
from the activities of our body. So our body (specifically our brain)
produces our mind – rather like a steam train puffs along emitting

steam: our thoughts are like 'puffs of smoke' that come from our mind. This means that our body causes our thoughts (the 'puffs of smoke') but our thoughts cannot affect our body in any way.

Solution 5: When we talk about our mind (our hopes, our dreams, our beliefs) we are in actual fact simply talking about certain types of behaviour, that is, the way we act in particular contexts. The meaning of all mental terms can in fact be converted into terms that simply describe our behaviour, although often it would be very long-winded to do this. For example, to say Percy has a toothache is really to say that he is holding his jaw, groaning, searching for aspirin and making an appointment with the dentist. It is not to say he has some thing, the pain, going on inside him which is causing all these outwardly observable behaviours. So we carry on talking about mental events (hopes, beliefs, pains, etc.) as if they actually exist as separate entities from our behaviour, but ultimately they are just a short-hand way of talking about behaviour.

■ Descartes' attempted solution: the pineal gland and animal spirits

We have seen that Descartes understands the mechanism of interaction to take place via the pineal gland and that motor and sensory information is communicated to and from the body via a very subtle material substance termed 'animal spirits'. In this way, Descartes appears to be trying to solve his problem. If the mind is unextended, then the point of contact with the body must be vanishingly small, so a small gland located in the centre of the brain is a good candidate. And the animal spirits, being so fine as almost to be spiritual, Descartes hopes can function half as matter, half as mind: a kind of intermediary allowing communication between the two worlds.

▶ criticism ◀ But neither of these strategies is going to work. For as we have already seen, if the mind is unextended, it doesn't matter how small the point of contact is supposed to be, *any* size is too big, since something with no size cannot make contact with anything. Moreover, the appeal to animal spirits fails to address the real difficulty. For animal spirits must be *either* material or spiritual. But if they are material we still need an account of how they interact with the mind, and if they are spiritual we still need an account of how they interact with the body, and so they succeed only in displacing the problem. In fact Descartes clearly thinks of them as material since they are extended, so no matter how refined they are thought to be, the manner of their communication with the mind remains a mystery.

■ Problem of intermingling

▶ criticism ◀ In order to enlighten us on the nature of the relationship Descartes speaks of the two substances being 'compounded and intermingled' (p. 159). In admitting this, Descartes is making a concession to the brute fact of human experience: we just don't seem to be two substances. 'I am not lodged in my body, like a pilot in his ship, but … I am joined to it very closely and indeed so compounded and intermingled with my body, that I form, as it were, a single whole with it' (p. 159). But we may wonder how it can possibly be, if I am unextended, that I can feel myself to be extended throughout my body. How can a mind without parts be 'intermingled' with a body? Surely to mix two things together, both need to be extended in space. If I blend flour and butter, both need to be divisible. So the mind surely would be unable to mingle with the body. Now, Descartes may reply that the idea of intermingling is just a metaphor but, if so, it is a metaphor which sheds no light on how mind and body can become fused in this way so that they seem to be one. In the absence of any account of how this can be, the lived experience of ourselves as embodied creatures with which we are all familiar inevitably sits very uncomfortably with Descartes' dualism.

■ Neural dependence

▶ criticism ◀ A final difficulty for Descartes concerns the fact that our minds appear to be heavily reliant on our brains. Damage to the brain has a direct impact on mental functioning. If there is alcohol in the blood coursing round my brain, I have trouble doing arithmetic. A sharp blow to the head can produce unconsciousness. As the brain grows we become better at learning, and as we age and our brains begin to decay our memory and mental agility often deteriorate. Increasingly, modern techniques, such as magnetic resonance imaging, which enable us to observe the brain, show that identifiable parts of the brain are active when we are engaged in specific sorts of mental activity, from doing philosophy or mathematics to willing, imagining and sensing. How is Descartes to explain the apparent dependence of the mind on the brain?

Descartes has no real difficulty explaining how sensation depends on the brain. For, as we have seen, it is changes in the brain which are the immediate cause of sense-experience. However, remember that, for Descartes, philosophy and mathematics are the province of pure reason. So such activities, one might think, should be able to continue unhindered by any physical process. Descartes can defend dualism here by emphasising that the mind is, in this life, intimately conjoined to the body. There are laws governing how changes in the brain impact on the mind, which account for the effects of drink and drugs, ageing, brain damage and so on, not just on bodily sensations but on higher mental functions. So even the ability to perform the *cogito* and think through a difficult philosophical argument using clear and distinct ideas – activities which occur in pure thought – can be influenced by the body. The mind is sullied by its association with our physical self and so can be hindered by it.

▶ criticism ◀   Nonetheless, while Descartes can accommodate the facts, they surely don't sit well with his theory. Why, on a dualist account, should unconsciousness follow from a blow to the head? Surely the brain might suffer trauma and we should remain conscious, since our conscious mind is supposed to be indestructible? Why do our mental abilities develop and deteriorate with age? Surely if our mind is simple our mental faculties should be as advanced at birth as at maturity or in our dotage? Why when drunk do I have trouble doing sums? Surely it should be possible to shut myself off from the body and do maths in the purity of my own thinking? These facts about the human condition are surely far better explained by the idea that our minds are the product of our brains.

■ Life after death

A final point to note is that Descartes' account of the mind–body relationship is supposed to allow for the separation of the mind from the body at our death. Consistent with Christian teaching, Descartes' dualism allows that, when the body decomposes, the mind, which cannot be decomposed because it is unitary and simple, will survive in order to be reunited with the body at the general resurrection. What life might be like without a body in the meantime is not explored in the *Meditations*. Presumably, the mind would no longer experience sensation. Could we still imagine? Perhaps we could still dream of things experienced in our previous life. But without senses it is difficult to see how we could communicate with any other minds that there might be, unless by some kind of telepathy. Whether we could still experience desire and emotion is unclear, depending on whether we suppose these to be a product of the union of mind and body, or something more purely spiritual. Presumably as a pure intellect we could be reasonably confident of being able to continue to contemplate **153** mathematical truths, to reason and philosophise, perhaps even more easily, now that we would no longer be adulterated with the body, which may be some consolation.

▶ criticism ◀ Whether or not one would have reason to look forward to such a state is one question, but another is whether we are really able to make coherent sense of it. It is certainly difficult to imagine what consciousness could be like without a body or sense organs. Without any sense-experiences could we really be aware of anything at all? Indeed, we may argue that a body is an essential element of who I am, and without it I would cease to be. Certainly in everyday life we identify people by their bodies. Losing the odd limb is one thing, but can we really make sense of the idea of someone surviving the loss of their whole body? We would not be in a position to communicate with someone in such a situation, nor to recognise or identify them. Moreover, the idea of disembodied consciousness sits uneasily with the facts of the neural dependence of many mental processes that we have discussed, in particular memory. For if my memories are encoded in my brain and when I die my brain decomposes, it seems I would be unable to carry any memories into the afterlife. But with no memories of my former life, it is unclear how I could meaningfully be considered the same person. In any case, Descartes doesn't involve himself in such speculation in the *Meditations*, so there is no need for us to pursue such questions here.[34]

Chapter 9

What you need to know about *Meditation 6* – the proof of the existence of matter; Cartesian dualism:

1 Descartes begins *Meditation 6* by clarifying the distinction between his faculty of imagination and his intellect. He conducts a thought experiment in which he tries to imagine many-sided shapes and concludes that his imagination is unable to make precise images of these in his mind. However, he notes, his intellect is perfectly able to understand the essential nature of such shapes. Since his intellect and imagination have different capacities, he concludes that they are distinct faculties.

2 Not only are they distinct, however, but the intellect is an essential mode of my mind, while the imagination is inessential. This is shown from the fact that I would be the same mind if I did not have the power to imagine, but I would not if I didn't have the power to reason and understand, as in such a case I would not be able to recognise that I exist.

3 Since the imagination is inessential to me, its origin is not within me and so the question arises as to where it comes from. Descartes conjectures that it comes from sensation: it is because I first experience the appearance of physical things through perception that I am then able to imagine them when I am not perceiving them.

4 Next Descartes enquires as to where sensations might come from. He argues that they cannot come from within him because he is unable to control them. But if they were part of his essential nature they would be subject to his will. Moreover, sensations are the appearance of extended things; and yet the mind is unextended. It follows from his causal principle that his mind cannot be the cause of his sensations.

5 What this shows is that sensations originate in a power outside of his mind. But what is this power? Two possibilities present themselves. Either they come from material objects as they had always seemed to, or they come directly from God. Descartes rejects the idea that they might come from God, since this would make God a deceiver, and so Descartes can conclude that they come from matter.

6 Descartes is now in a position to give an account of the true nature of material reality. He claims that it possesses only those qualities which we clearly and distinctly perceive it to have, as God would not deceive us about such qualities. This means that matter has those properties that

can be described in the language of geometry and mathematics, namely position, number, size, shape, duration and motion.

7 However, the colours, smells, sounds and tastes which I also perceive are confused perceptions, since such properties cannot be rendered mathematically. This means that I can have no real idea what it is that causes them simply by analysing the experiences. So the powers that cause these sensations are caused by the arrangements of the minute part of objects of which I am not directly aware.

8 Having proved the existence of matter, Descartes now argues that his own body is distinct from his mind, on the grounds that his mind is clearly and distinctly perceived to be an unextended thinking thing, and that his body is clearly and distinctly perceived to be an extended unthinking thing. Things with different essences must be distinct things, so I am not my body.

9 A second argument to the same conclusion focuses on the fact that the mind is indivisible, i.e. I cannot divide my consciousness. By contrast, however, my body, being an extended object, is necessarily divisible into parts.

10 Descartes concludes the *Meditation* by outlining the nature of the relationship between the mind and the body. Although they are distinct substances, in this life they are in causal interaction. The mind can affect the body through acts of will and the body can affect the mind through the processes of external and internal perception.

11 Descartes conjectures that the mind and body interact via the pineal gland and that motor and sensory information is communicated around the body along the nerves by means of animal spirits. The two substances are experienced in this life as an intimate union so that we feel ourselves to be as one with our bodies.

The legacy of the *Meditations*

Rationalism

Some readers, after initial excitement during the first two *Meditations*, can feel somewhat disenchanted with the direction the work then takes. After being drawn in by the method of doubt, the reader then follows Descartes on his seemingly flawless journey to the *cogito*. But from this position, after tentatively concluding he is a thinking thing, Descartes attempts to prove the existence of God. And here the reader's doubts about Descartes' arguments tend to creep in and the *Meditations* lose their air of faultlessly reasoned argument.

It is important to remember, though, that the feeling of disappointment that some readers experience says as much about the brilliance of the first two *Meditations* as it does about any flaws in reasoning from then on. The sceptical scenarios of the Dream and Evil Demon Arguments grab the attention of the reader and undermine our confidence in our knowledge as much as they do Descartes'. It is not just Descartes' life that might be an illusion, but our own. Can Descartes really overcome such a radical and seemingly devastating scepticism? The intrigue of the *Meditations* lies in the fact that we feel a personal involvement in his quest: his need to discover some certainties in the sea of doubts is also ours. The genius of the *cogito* seems to provide some initial hope and any subsequent disillusionment hints at the enduring appeal of the rationalist project and the idea that through reason alone we can reveal certainties about the world.

Up to this point philosophy had never been approached in quite this manner. From a cabin shut off from the world, ignoring everything he thinks he has learned hitherto, Descartes is attempting to ascertain what can be known about the universe and the condition of man, through the use of reason alone. Although his project is generally considered to have failed – that is, failed to establish much beyond the *cogito* – his work inspired a host of other philosophers to pick up the baton of reason and see how far they could run with it.

The whole philosophical approach which aspires to establishing substantive truths without appeal to empirical information became known as rationalism and two of the key philosophers who followed Descartes within this tradition were Baruch Spinoza (1632–1677) and Gottfried Wilhelm Leibniz (1646–1716).

Spinoza took the notion of rational method to an extreme. He attempted to prove his philosophical claims by organising them, in the manner of Euclid, in the form of an axiomatic system. He started by setting out a series of definitions and axioms, for example:

Definition:

I. By that which is self-caused, I mean that of which the essence involves existence, or that of which the nature is only conceivable as existent.

Axiom:

I. Everything which exists, exists either in itself or in something else.

Spinoza then went on to set out a whole series of propositions, laying out a proof for each one:

PROP. III. Things which have nothing in common cannot be one the cause of the other.

Proof.—If they have nothing in common, it follows that one cannot be apprehended by means of the other (Ax. v.), and, therefore, one cannot be the cause of the other. (Ax. iv.). Q.E.D.[35]

In proving the series of propositions a strange and unique account of the world emerges, apparently unearthed through the use of reason alone. There is just one substance; God did not create the universe, rather they are the same thing. God has an infinite number of attributes or modes, of which physical extension and thought are the two that humans know. Mind and matter, then, are not two substances, but two modes of the one substance. The universe and all that happens is completely determined, and so on.

Rationalism in the manner of Spinoza is generally considered to have failed. Outside the world of mathematics it seems there is little that can be proved about reality by unaided reason. The universe could well have been different from the way it is. In other words, it is a contingent matter that things are arranged as they are and so the only way we can find out the exact nature of the universe is to observe how it behaves, and only then reason about it. Science progresses not by pure reason about how the world must be, but by reason in tandem with observation of how it actually is.

It should be noted that the term 'rationalism' was coined long after Descartes' life and it is a term that perhaps doesn't fit Descartes' views as well as it does other philosophers'. Indeed, Descartes himself would probably not have described himself a rationalist. However, his importance in the world of philosophy is such that he is considered one of the key figures of the movement.

Modern philosophy

Although the rationalist project may not have succeeded, some of its elements have had a lasting impact on philosophy. The rationalist conviction that substantive knowledge can be reached by reason alone involves the claim that there is a proper approach or method for reaching the truth. The idea of establishing a proper methodology for philosophy, as well as for science, was one of Descartes' central aims.

As discussed in the introduction, the emphasis on questions of method is a key turning point in the history of philosophy. Although philosophers previously had discussed their methods, these methods were often borne out by their prior beliefs and convictions about the world. Their concern with method – in other words their epistemology – was not a central part of their philosophy, and in many cases was derived from their beliefs about what was real or what existed, in other words, from their ontology. But with Descartes we see epistemology being placed at the heart of philosophical endeavour. Questions of method, knowledge and truth came to be addressed before other philosophical questions could be properly tackled. This approach to philosophy is very much alive today.

The mind-body distinction

Descartes' account of the nature of the mind and body has also left a lasting legacy on western thought. Descartes did not invent dualism, indeed it is not likely that any single person did. Different forms of dualism are implicit in the early writings of many cultures, and evidence for the belief can be traced back to before the written word. Ceremonial burial, for example, indicates some kind of belief in an afterlife, which in turn may suggest a belief in a world beyond the physical. Although implicit in many religions, most early accounts of dualism are vague and lack any philosophical precision. In the Bible St Paul speaks vaguely of the soul being reunited at the

general resurrection with a new spiritual body, but admits that
we cannot yet understand how this will happen.[36] Within
western philosophy we can trace dualism back at least as far as
Plato who offers some of the first serious philosophical
arguments in its favour.[37]

In the thirteenth century Thomas Aquinas' efforts to marry
the works of Aristotle with the teachings of the Bible led him
to produce a more developed account of the relationship
between mind and body. This was no mean feat, as Aristotle
had not believed the soul could live on after the demise of the
body. Aristotle regarded the soul as the 'form' of the body.
To understand his idea consider a wax statue of Winston
Churchill. In this instance the 'form' is the shape that the
matter of the wax takes. If the statue melts the matter takes
on a new shape and so the original form is lost. In such a case
it clearly makes no sense to think of the old shape of the
statue as somehow living on. The form and the matter cannot
be separated. In the same way Aristotle argued that our souls
are what give form to the matter which is our bodies. Here
the idea is not simply that of giving shape to the body as in
the statue example, but of animating it and making us what
we are as human beings. On this view the soul cannot live on
after the demise of the body, as the form cannot exist
independently of the matter. They are not two separate
substances. Aquinas' acceptance of this idea means that he
believed the human person could only be complete once the
soul and body had been reunited at the general resurrection.
Departing from Aristotle somewhat, Aquinas does believe the
soul exists between death and resurrection, but nonetheless
argues that in this condition it does not constitute the whole
self. I am only a full person again once I am reunited with
a body.

It is noteworthy that it is *not* Aquinas' account of a soul
that will be familiar to many people in the Christian West.
The fact that this is no longer the dominant conception of the
soul is largely the responsibility of Descartes. The account of
the mind provided in the *Meditations* as the essence of the
self, as something each of us is directly aware of when we look
inwards, as the agency behind our actions and as something
that can exist completely independently of the body, has
become embedded in western thought to the extent that it
has been referred to as the 'official' doctrine of the mind and
body.[38] This conception may not have been totally in keeping
with Aquinas' doctrine as accepted by the Church, but it did
have a certain appeal to the ordinary reader. Many of us feel
as if our minds are somehow non-material; after all, thoughts
do not seem to occupy space, and it seems impossible to

explain our thoughts and emotions in physical terms. It also chimes with our ordinary sense that the mind is the cause of our behaviour.

Descartes and science

In Descartes' day, the Church saw science as a threat to its teachings about the world, and Descartes' clear distinction between mind and body was important in helping, if not to resolve, at least to take some of the sting out of this conflict. The physical world, according to Descartes, is unthinking and extended. It has properties that can be measured, examined and studied. The mind on the other hand does not occupy space and so is beyond the prying reach of the scientist. This separation allows room for both science and the Church to operate side by side without encroaching on each other's territory. The physical world is viewed as a machine, whose workings can be revealed by science, and the mental world – the world of thoughts, conscience, morality and desires – can be the domain of religion.

As we saw in the introduction, Descartes was part of the new wave of scientists whose approach involved explaining the world using relatively few properties, rather than the multitude used by the Aristotelian scientists of the day. In Descartes' opinion, all events and phenomena in the natural world could (in theory) be explained by reference to just matter and its size, shape, motion, duration and quantity. We can see that this approach, in essence, turned out to be the way that science would move forward. The property of being hot or cold is now explained by reference to motion of atoms and molecules. The property of sound is explained by reference to the motion of compression of waves of air. Scientists 'reduce' the myriad of properties that we observe in the world around us to the interaction of a few basic measurable elements, i.e. matter and a handful of forces. It was Descartes, in part, who helped to sow the seeds for this new approach to natural science by insisting that what was real in matter was what could be clearly and distinctly understood – in other words, what could be dealt with mathematically – and so was amenable to measurement.

Ironically, it is this same approach that is now used to explain the properties of thought and consciousness. Whereas Descartes saw the need to posit the existence of both matter *and* mind, many modern philosophers would reject this approach. Just as with heat and sound, they would claim that thought itself can be explained in terms of matter and its movements.

Phenomenology

'Phenomenology' is the term given to one of the most important philosophical schools of the twentieth century. Its literal meaning is the study (-*ology*) of appearances (*phenomena*) and its method of doing philosophy begins by an examination of the way the world appears in our conscious mind.

Phenomenology takes as its starting point the position Descartes reaches with his *cogito* argument. At this stage Descartes is aware that he exists, that he has a mind and that his mind has various modes; in other words, that he is aware of thinking, feeling, sensing and so on. What he does not yet know is where these experiences come from; in particular he doesn't know whether his sensations are the product of a material world, or simply some sort of dream. His sense-experience may be produced by an evil demon, after all. At this point the phenomenologist, rather than trying to dismiss the demon and to prove the existence of material objects, takes a different route to Descartes. The phenomenologist simply tries to describe how the world *appears* to the mind, thus avoiding questions of whether the world and its objects actually exist. As it is often put, phenomenology 'brackets' the existence of the world in order to focus on the way things appear. Objects, feelings, emotions, and so on, all appear to the mind, regardless of whether they are caused by matter, dreams or a demon; and so it is possible to examine and explore them as such. So phenomenologists see the role of philosophy as the effort to describe the world as it appears to a conscious mind. Although Descartes would not be described as a phenomenologist, the movement was in large measure inspired by the *Meditations* and acknowledges the importance of Descartes in its writings.[39]

Conclusion

We can see from the above, the legacy of Descartes, and of the *Meditations* in particular, is vast. The book stands at a turning point in history, when the revolutionary new science was starting to explain the world in exciting and fruitful ways. Descartes was at the forefront of this change. He stands between the traditional Platonic and Aristotelian ways of doing philosophy and the new modern approaches of rationalism and empiricism. For these reasons Descartes' work is said to herald the modern era of philosophy.

Glossary

This glossary explains the meanings of some of the terminology used by Descartes in the *Meditations* as well as philosophical terms used in this book when explaining his ideas.

ACCIDENTS An accident is a particular instantiation of a **mode** of a **substance**. So the accidents of the **intellect** (which is a mode of mind-substance) will be examples of particular thoughts. Similarly, the accidents of **extension** (which is a mode of matter) will be the particular sizes and shapes a material object has.

ACTUAL REALITY See **formal reality**.

A POSTERIORI A Latin term describing those **beliefs** or **knowledge** claims that can only be known through experience of the world; for example, to know that the Atlantic is smaller than the Pacific some **empirical** investigation is necessary. *A posteriori* beliefs are contrasted with *a priori* beliefs which can be known independently of experience.

A PRIORI A Latin term describing those beliefs or knowledge claims that can be known prior to or independently of experience; for example, that '1,000,000 + 1 = 1,000,001' can be known without actually counting a million apples, adding another one, and then recounting them. *A priori* beliefs are contrasted with *a posteriori* beliefs, which are ones that must be derived from experience.

ANALYTIC AND SYNTHETIC An analytic **proposition** is one that is true purely in virtue of the meanings of the terms used to express it. In other words, an analytic truth is one that is true by definition: for example, 'A bachelor is an unmarried man.' In this case, simply by *analysing* or unpacking the meanings of the words involved we can come to see that it has to be true. Analytic truths are contrasted with synthetic truths, i.e. truths that cannot be determined simply by analysing the meanings of the terms used. For example, 'All bachelors

have the use of at least one kidney' is a synthetic truth, since having the use of a kidney is not part of the concept of being a bachelor.

ARGUMENT An argument is a series of **propositions** intended to support a **conclusion**. The propositions offered in support of the conclusion are termed **premises**.

BELIEF A belief is a claim about the world. If I believe a **proposition**, then I assent to its being true. But beliefs are not guaranteed to be true. We can have false beliefs, and this is one way in which beliefs differ from **knowledge**, for if I know something then what I know must be true.

BODY The term 'body' is used by Descartes to refer to any physical object, but it is also used to refer to one object in particular, namely the body he calls his own. His idea of his body is that of a 'machine of flesh and bones' (p. 104).

CARTESIAN Of or relating to Descartes. 'Cartesian' is the term used to describe ideas which originate with him. So Cartesian dualism is Descartes' theory of **mind** and **body**, and **Cartesian doubt** is Descartes' sceptical method.

CARTESIAN CIRCLE The Cartesian Circle is the fallacy that Descartes allegedly makes in the *Meditations* in his efforts to establish the reliability of **clear and distinct** ideas and to prove the existence of **God**. The charge is that Descartes' reasoning is circular: in other words he presupposes in the **premises** of his **argument** what he sets out to prove in the **conclusion**. Descartes needs to establish that **judgements** made clearly and distinctly can be guaranteed to be true so that he can found his system of **knowledge**. To do this he needs to prove the existence of a non-deceiving God who will guarantee the **veracity** of such judgements. But in order to prove the existence of such a God he has to rely on judgements the **truth** of which is only guaranteed because they are clearly and distinctly recognised as such. But since their clarity and distinctness hasn't yet been established as a guarantee of their truth, he cannot presuppose that they are clear and distinct in his argument for God's existence. In other words, he presupposes that clear and distinct judgements are reliable in order to prove that they are.

CARTESIAN DOUBT OR PHILOSOPHICAL DOUBT This is Descartes' sceptical method, used to find certainty and what we have referred to as the 'method of doubt' or 'theoretical doubt'. Unlike doubt as used in everyday life, where we doubt a **belief** when we have good reasons to think it may be false, Descartes' doubt involves withholding assent from a belief if it is in any way possible it could be false, no matter how unlikely. Descartes is not saying that he actually believes most or all of his beliefs are false; rather he is suspending **judgement** about them until any can be established as beyond possible doubt. Such beliefs will then be used as the foundation for establishing **knowledge**.

CLEAR AND DISTINCT A **belief** or **judgement** that is recognised clearly and distinctly is one which can be 'intuited' by the **mind** by means of **reason** alone. A clear and distinct belief is a simple truth which can be known in a single moment or act of **understanding**. Part of Descartes' idea here is that a judgement made in this way is one which is well illuminated, as it were, by what he calls the '**light of reason**', that is to say it is *clear*. And at the same time, because it is simple and so cannot be broken down into further steps, it is not confused with any other ideas, and so is *distinct*. Descartes' examples of clear and distinct beliefs are the basic claims of logic, geometry and mathematics as well as the self-knowledge gained through the *cogito*. Knowledge of such truths, it is claimed, resists any sceptical attack, since we recognise their truth immediately and without room for doubt or error. For example, it is in vain to ask how I know that triangles have three sides. Such easy and simple knowledge is given in the very act of understanding the terms involved. There is no further evidence I need appeal to in order to justify it.

COGITO (the) Latin for 'I think', and shorthand for Descartes' famous **argument** to prove his own existence. Descartes attempted to doubt that he existed, but realised that, in order to doubt this, he must exist, so his own existence was **indubitable**.

CONCLUSION The claim that an **argument** tries to prove; and which is supported by its **premises**.

CORPOREAL Of or relating to physical bodies; having a material rather than spiritual nature. A 'corporeal object' is a material thing and Descartes claims the **essence** of all such bodies is **extension**.

DEDUCTION A deductive **argument** is one where the **truth** of the **conclusion** is guaranteed by the truth of the **premises**, so if the premises are true the conclusion must also be true. In other words, the conclusion is entailed by the premises. For example, from the premise that all ravens are black it follows necessarily that if you encounter a raven it will be black. Deduction is the process of reasoning by which we move from the premises of deductive arguments to their conclusions and stands in contrast to **induction**.

DOUBT See **Cartesian doubt**.

DUALISM Dualism about **mind** and **body** is the claim that humans are made of two distinct kinds of stuff or **substance**: a material body and a spiritual mind.

DUBITABLE A **belief** which is dubitable is capable of being doubted.

EMPIRICAL Of or relating to experience. Empirical knowledge is knowledge gained through experience or experiment (see *a posteriori*).

EMPIRICISM An **epistemological** position which holds that our **beliefs** and **knowledge** must be based on experience. It also claims that our concepts or ideas must derive from our experience.

ENLIGHTENMENT The development in seventeenth- and eighteenth-century European thought characterised by a renewed confidence in humanity's ability to acquire **knowledge** by the use of **reason**.

EPISTEMOLOGY/EPISTEMOLOGICAL Epistemology is the theory of **knowledge**. This term is derived from the Ancient Greek words *episteme* meaning 'knowledge' and *logos* meaning 'account', or 'rationale'.

ESSENCE That which makes a thing the specific thing it is. If it were to lose any part of its essence or any essential **modes** or properties, then it would no longer be the thing in question. For example, having three sides is part of what makes a triangle a triangle. Having three sides is therefore an essential property of being a triangle, and if it lost or gained a side, it would no longer be a triangle.

EXTENSION/EXTENDED Extension means occupying physical space. Descartes claimed that all matter is extended, meaning that it has three spatial dimensions. Descartes also claimed that thoughts were not extended, meaning they do not occupy physical space but exist only in time.

FALLACY A fallacy is any flawed **argument**. Many fallacies are common enough to have been given names, for example, the masked-man fallacy (see pages 137–8).

FORMAL REALITY Descartes uses the terms 'formal' or 'actual' reality to denote the degree of perfection possessed by actual things. **Substances** have greater formal reality than **modes**, since the latter depend upon the former.

FOUNDATIONALISM The view about the structure of **justification** which claims that there are two sorts of **belief**: those which are basic or foundational and which require no justification (or which are self-justifying), and those which are built on top of the foundations and justified in terms of them. In Descartes' system the foundations are beliefs which can be clearly and distinctly recognised as true.

GOD Descartes defines God as a being 'who is all powerful and by whom I was created and made as I am' (p. 98); 'who is sovereign, eternal, infinite, unchangeable, all-knowing, all-powerful and universal Creator of all things outside himself' (p. 119) whose 'nature … is immense, incomprehensible and infinite' (p. 134) and a 'supremely perfect being' (p. 144). The **Ontological** Argument claims that necessary existence is also part of the very idea or definition of God.

HYPERBOLIC Deliberately exaggerated. Used to refer to Descartes' extreme form of **scepticism**, as in 'hyperbolic doubt'.

I (THE) The self or **mind**: that which is conscious of its own existence.

IMAGINATION Descartes writes: '… imagining is nothing other than contemplating the figure or image of a **corporeal** object' (p. 106), in other words, it is the ability to visualise physical objects before our mind's eye, as, for example, if you imagine a cow jumping over the moon.

IMMATERIAL Not made of matter. Since the **essence** of matter is **extension** in space, according to Descartes, immaterial substance does not occupy space. The 'I' or conscious **mind** is said to be immaterial in this sense.

IMMUTABLE Something that can never change.

IMPULSE/INSTINCT Descartes is aware that most of the **beliefs** we form in everyday life are not grounded in **clear and distinct** ideas. We do not form our beliefs by the careful methods of the **Cartesian** meditator; rather we are impelled to make rash **judgements** by our instinctive nature. For example, we are led by our instincts to believe we have a **body** and that we are surrounded by other physical bodies which really possess various qualities, from shapes and sizes through to colours and sounds. However, while nature has impelled us to form these beliefs, it is not the safest method for acquiring **knowledge**. Such a method of belief formation may be useful in helping us to survive, but it is *blind* with respect to uncovering the **truth**. Descartes' *Meditations* are in large part an attempt to show that by use of our **intellect** and **intuition**, operating in the light of **reason**, we can establish a true and accurate picture of reality and correct some of the beliefs acquired by our blind impulses.

INDUBITABLE A **belief** which is indubitable is impossible to doubt.

INDUCTION An inductive **argument** is one which **reasons** from particular **premises** to a general conclusion, for example, inferring from particular examples (every raven I've seen has been black) to a generalisation (all ravens are black). Note that in an inductive argument the truth of the conclusion is not fully guaranteed by the truth of the premises. See also **deduction**.

INTELLECT The faculty of the **mind** or **mode** of consciousness which enables us to reason, variously termed the '**understanding**', 'reason', 'intellection', 'conception' and 'the power of conceiving' by Descartes in the Penguin translation. In this book we have confined ourselves to the terms 'intellect' and 'understanding' when referring to this faculty.

INTUITION   Intuition is a kind of mental seeing by which rational truths can be recognised. For Descartes the mind deploys its intuition when it sees by the '**light of reason**' that $2 + 2 = 4$ or that a sphere is bounded by one surface. Contrast this with blind **impulse** or instinct.

JUDGEMENT   A **belief** or decision to believe. In making a judgement the **mind** affirms a belief to be true. Only when we make judgements is it possible to make errors or come to hold false beliefs. So if we suspend judgement we can be sure of not falling into error, hence Descartes' method of doubt. Descartes argues that it is the **will** which makes judgements, and because the will can make them based on inadequate evidence it is quite possible to acquire false beliefs. However, if we rein in our will and confine ourselves to making judgements which we clearly and distinctly recognise to be sound we can avoid making errors. For example, the judgement that objects really contain colours is a rash one based on a blind **impulse** or **instinct**, not a **clear and distinct** one made by the **intellect**.

JUSTIFICATION   The support or grounds for a **belief** which gives someone a reason for believing it.

KNOWLEDGE   To know something is, at the least, to believe a proposition which is true. Traditionally a knowledge claim is also thought to require adequate **justification** in support of it.

LIGHT OF REASON   In the metaphorics common to Descartes' time, truths that could be clearly understood by the **mind** involved a kind of intellectual seeing or '**intuition**', and this seeing is facilitated by the 'light of reason'. So understanding a simple geometric **truth**, for example, is possible for humans because we have this faculty of intuition and because such truths are illuminated by a kind of rational light. Truths well lit by this light are said to be 'clear' and if they are not confused with any other ideas they are 'distinct'.

MATERIAL   Made of physical matter. According to Descartes, this involved occupying physical space. In contrast, the '**I**' or **mind** is thought of by Descartes as *immaterial*.

MIND   The mind is 'a thing that thinks ... that is to say, a thing that doubts, perceives, affirms, denies, wills, does not will, that imagines also, and which feels' (p. 107). So, it is the conscious self and includes anything of which you are immediately aware. Descartes identifies the **mind** with the '**I**' and **Cartesian** dualism consists in the claim that the mind or self is distinct from the **body**.

MODE   A mode is an attribute or property of a **substance**. Descartes argues that the **intellect**, **will**, **imagination** and **sensation** are all modes of his conscious **mind**. Size and shape are modes of matter.

OBJECTIVE REALITY   Ideas are representations or 'pictures' of things. So an idea of a cat is a representation of a cat, and it can be thought of in this way regardless of whether any cats actually exist. Descartes reckons that we can rank our ideas according to the perfection they have as representations, which is to say, in terms of their objective reality. So my idea of a cat will have greater objective reality than my idea of the colour ginger, since the colour depends on the cat. One is the idea of a **substance**, the other of a **mode**, and since modes depend on substances they are less perfect. Objective reality is a quality of ideas and is contrasted with **formal reality**, which is a quality of things.

OMNIPOTENT   All-powerful.

OMNISCIENT   All-knowing.

ONTOLOGY/ONTOLOGICAL   Ontology is the study of existence. If you were to write down everything you thought existed (cats, dogs, electrons, aliens, etc), then this list would form your own personal ontology. If aliens were present on the list then you could be said to be making an 'ontological commitment' to the existence of aliens (in other words, you claim they exist). The Ontological Argument is a particular proof of God's existence, used in the *Meditations*, which tries to show that the very meaning of the concept '**God**' implies that he must exist.

PERCEPTION   In the Penguin translation 'perception' and 'perceiving' are used to refer to the conscious experience of **sensations** as they appear in the **mind**. '... it is very certain that it seems to me that I see light, hear a noise and feel heat, and this is properly what in me is called perceiving' (p. 107). There are external perceptions such as when we perceive light and sounds, but also internal ones such as pain and hunger. The verb 'to perceive' is used more generally by Descartes to mean whatever the **mind** experiences or understands and so is not confined to what is sensed, as when he speaks of the **intellect** or **understanding** 'perceiving' a **truth**.

PRECONDITION   A precondition is something that must be true, occur or exist, in order for something else to be true, occur or exist. For example, a precondition of playing a football match is that there is a football. Another precondition for the match would be that there were teams. Without these elements a football match could not occur, so a ball and teams are preconditions of a football match.

PREDICATE   Many **propositions** can be divided into a **subject** and a predicate, where the subject is the thing that the proposition is about and the predicate gives us information about the subject. For example, in the sentence 'The balloon is red', 'is red' is the predicate, and 'The balloon' is the subject. Descartes' **Ontological** Argument involves the claim that, in the sentence '**God** exists', 'exists' is a predicate applying to 'God'. However, philosophers from Kant onwards have doubted whether existence is a genuine predicate and have used this claim to criticise the Ontological Argument.

PREMISE   A statement or claim used to support the **conclusion** of an **argument**.

PRIMARY AND SECONDARY QUALITIES
According to the **representative realist** theory of **perception** the qualities we perceive in physical objects fall into two classes: the primary qualities such as size and shape, and secondary qualities such as colours, sounds and smells. Primary qualities exist in the objects themselves pretty much as they appear to, but the secondary qualities are really powers to produce **sensations** in us, and so the way these are perceived is not an accurate representation of what is causing them. These powers are a product of the arrangement of the parts of the object which are too small for us to observe. Descartes draws this distinction by arguing that our perception of physical objects can be divided into those qualities which are amenable to mathematical and geometric description and those that are not. Of the former, we have a **clear and distinct understanding**, meaning that we are able to understand what it is for an object to have such a quality. I have a clear and distinct understanding of what it is for a ball to be round and so my idea of roundness is an accurate representation of the real shape of the ball. However, those qualities which are not readily described in geometry and mathematics, such as smells and colours, I have

no clear and distinct understanding of. This means I have no real idea of what it is for an object to smell of violets or be pink. So my perception of these qualities is obscure and confused; in other words, they are not accurate representations of what is causing them.

PROPOSITION   A proposition is what is asserted by the kind of sentence that makes a claim about the way the world is: for example, 'there is a cat on my mat' or 'I am thinking about a dragon'. Other sentences can play different roles: for example, 'Sit down now!' or 'What are you looking at?' Such sentences (commands, questions, exclamations) do not make specific claims about the way the world is, and hence do not express propositions.

RATIONALISM   The tendency in philosophy to regard **reason**, as opposed to sense experience, as the primary source of the important **knowledge** of which we are capable. Rationalists also tend to argue that many concepts are innate as opposed to acquired from experience. Rationalists are typically impressed by the systematic nature of mathematical knowledge and the possibility of certainty that it affords and attempt to extend this type of knowledge into other areas of human enquiry, such as to knowledge of the physical world, or to ethics. Rationalism is traditionally contrasted with **empiricism**: the view that most of what we know is acquired through experience.

REASON   The capacity for rational **argument** and **judgement**. The process by which we are able to discover the **truth** of things by pure thought, by inferring **conclusions** from **premises**. Often contrasted with **instinct**, emotion or **imagination**.

REPRESENTATIVE REALISM   The theory of **perception** which claims that we perceive the physical world only indirectly via mental representations which appear in our minds. These representations are the **sensations** caused by the impact of physical objects upon our sense organs. It is on the basis of the appearance of these sensations that we make **judgements** about the existence and nature of objects beyond our minds.

SCEPTICISM   Philosophical scepticism entails raising doubts about our claims to know. The purpose of scepticism in philosophy is firstly to test our knowledge claims. If they can survive the sceptic's attack, then they vindicate themselves as genuine. Descartes used scepticism in this way so that he could isolate a few certainties which he felt could be used as a foundation to rebuild a body of knowledge free from doubt or error (see **Cartesian doubt**).

SELF-VERIFYING   A **proposition** or thought that proves its own **truth** is said to be self-verifying. For example, 'There are more than eight words in the English language' is a proposition that proves the truth of what it is claiming in the very process of being written or read. Descartes' *cogito* argument is self-verifying in this sense.

SENSATION   A sense experience as it appears to the mind, such as an 'internal' sensation of hunger or an 'external' sensation of sound. Here we use this term interchangeably with **perception**.

SOLIPSISM   The sceptical difficulty of being sure of one's own mind's existence, but not being able to establish the existence of anything beyond one's own mind.

SOUL   Traditionally the soul is considered to be the element of human beings that gives us life, that animates us and makes us conscious. In many religions and philosophies, the soul is thought to be the **essence** of our self and so what sustains our personal identity. Dualists regard the soul as **immaterial** and this means we can survive physical death. Descartes equates the soul with the **mind**.

SUBJECT   In grammar, the part of a **proposition** that picks out that which is being described or discussed. For example, in the proposition 'The red balloon popped' the subject is the balloon (see **predicate**). 'Subject' is also another word for that which thinks, i.e. the conscious self, **mind** or **I**.

SUBSTANCE   A substance is any stuff that can exist on its own and is not dependent on something else. Descartes' dualism is the claim that there are two kinds of substance in the universe: matter, which occupies space and does not think; and mind, which thinks and does not occupy space. (Strictly, though, since both of these substances are created by **God** and so ultimately dependent on him for their existence, there is only one true substance: God.) Other aspects of reality such as colours and shapes cannot exist by themselves but rely on substances in order to exist. These are termed 'properties', 'attributes', or in Descartes' terminology, **modes**.

SYLLOGISM   A syllogism is a three-line argument. Elements from the first two lines,

the **premises**, are combined to prove a third line, the **conclusion**. For example:

Premise 1   All mammals have hearts.
Premise 2   A dog is a mammal.
Conclusion   Therefore a dog has a heart.

SYNTHETIC   See **analytic and synthetic**.

TELEOLOGICAL   Deriving from the Greek word *telos* meaning purpose, goal or end, a teleological explanation is a way of accounting for events by reference to their purpose or ultimate goal. For example, a teleological explanation of a sprouting acorn will refer to the purpose of this event, or to the future state towards which it is aimed, such as the acorn's aim to become a tree, or its search for soil and water. Such a teleological approach may be contrasted with efficient or mechanical explanations, which explain events only by making reference to physical factors leading up to the event. For example, a mechanical explanation of the emerging shoot may make reference to the conditions which produce the development, such as changes in temperature and humidity, and the production of enzymes, leading to the growth of certain cells.

TRANSCENDENTAL ARGUMENT   A term coined by Kant to describe a certain form of anti-sceptical **argument**. A transcendental argument attempts to show that the sceptic must presuppose what they attempt to deny in order for their argument to make sense. In other words transcendental arguments try to show what **beliefs** must exist in order for doubt to take place. Such beliefs then transcend the possibility of doubt, because, for doubt to exist, they must be in place.

TRUTH   Truth is a quality possessed by **beliefs** and **propositions**, and a truth is a true belief or proposition. There are different accounts of what truth consists in. The correspondence theory, for example, says that a belief or **proposition** is true just if what it says about the world corresponds with the way things really are. In the *Meditations*, Descartes argues that a belief that can be recognised as true clearly and distinctly, or a belief about which there can be no doubt, must actually be true.

UNDERSTANDING   The **intellect**.

VERACITY   Truthfulness, accuracy.

WILL   The capacity of the **mind** freely to choose what to believe or do.

Notes

■ Chapter 2

1 *Discours de la Méthode*, Part IV, René Descartes, *Oeuvres de Descartes*, 11 vols, revised edition, ed. Charles Adam and Paul Tannery (Paris: Librairie Philosophique J. Vrin and Le Centre National de la Recherche Scientifique, 1964–1976). Henceforth noted as AT.

2 *Discourse 2, Discourse on Method and The Meditations*, tr. F. E. Sutcliffe, Penguin Classics, 1968.

3 Ibid.

4 Bernard Williams in Paul Edwards ed. *Encyclopaedia of Philosophy* (New York: Macmillan, 1967).

5 The argument outlined here is originally found in David Hume's *Treatise on Human Nature*, ed. Ernest C. Mossner (Harmondsworth: Penguin Classics, 1985).

6 Galileo, *Il Saggiatore* (1623).

7 *Discourse 1*, in *Discourse on Method and The Meditations*.

8 *Discourse 2*, ibid.

■ Chapter 4

9 *Discourse on Method*, trans. L. J. Lafleur, in *Philosophical Essays* (Indianapolis: Bobbs-Merrill, 1964), p. 18.

10 *Rules for the Direction of the Mind*, in *The Philosophical Works of Descartes*, Vol. 1, trans. E. S. Haldane and G. R. T. Ross (Cambridge University Press, 1911).

11 David Hume, *Enquiry* I, sect. 12, ed. T. L. Beauchamp (Oxford University Press, 1999) p. 199.

12 This simile is due to Otto Neurath. See 'Protocol Statements', in Otto Neurath, *Philosophical Papers 1913–1946*, ed. and trans. R. S. Cohen and M. Neurath (Dordrecht: Reidel, 1983).

13 This analogy adapted from B. Williams, *Descartes* (Harmondsworth: Penguin, 1978).

■ Chapter 5

14 AT, vii, 140, cf. v, 147.

15 *Discourse 4* in *Discourse on Method and The Meditations*.

16 Haldane and Ross, *The Philosophical Works of Descartes*, Vol. 2, p. 137.

17 B. Russell, *The Problems of Philosophy* (Oxford University Press, 1912), p. 8.

18 David Hume, *Treatise on Human Nature*, I, iv, 6.

19 Ludwig Wittgenstein, *Tractatus Logico-Philosophicus* 5.621–5.6331.

20 Haldane and Ross, *The Philosophical Works of Descartes*, Vol. 2, p. 25.

21 *The Philosophical Writings of Descartes*, trans. J. Cottingham, R. Stoothoff and D. Murdoch, Vols 1 and 2 (Cambridge University Press, 1948–85), 2, 276. Henceforth noted as CSM.

22 Descartes confirms this in the *Replies* where he says he takes for granted an understanding of what thinking etc. are.

23 See, for example, Etienne Bonnot de Condillac, *Treatise on Sensations* (1754) and the *Essay on the Origin of Human Knowledge* (1746). 'Descartes was right to think that to arrive at certain knowledge one had to begin by rejecting all we thought we had acquired, but he was wrong when he thought that to this end it would suffice to doubt. To doubt whether two and two are four, or if man is a rational animal, is to have the ideas of "two", "four", "man", "animal", and "rational". Doubt allows ideas to subsist as they are: thus, since error derives from our ideas having been badly formed, doubt could not prevent it.' *Essai sur l'origine des connoissance humaines*, p. 112, in *Oeuvres Philosophiques*, Vol. 1, ed. G. Le Roy, Corpus General des Philosophes Français, XXXIII, 3 vols (Paris: Presses Universitaires de France, 1947–51).

■ Chapter 7

24 AT X 368.
25 Note that here we are passing over Descartes' distinction between innate and adventitious ideas (p. 116).
26 Here we can ignore Descartes' distinction between 'actual or formal' and 'eminent' reality, the difference being that to possess something actually or formally is to actually possess it, while to possess something eminently is to be able to produce it in something else.
27 CSM II 130.
28 For example, Thomas Aquinas.

■ Chapter 8

29 For a more detailed discussion of Kant's objection and more recent developments in this area see G. Jones, D. Cardinal and J. Hayward, *Philosophy of Religion* (London: Hodder Murray, 2005).
30 CSM II 72, AT VII, 99.

■ Chapter 9

31 For a discussion of Berkeley's idealist theory of perception see D. Cardinal, J. Hayward and G. Jones, *Epistemology: The Theory of Knowledge* (London: John Murray, 2004) in this series, pp. 107ff.
32 See ibid. pp. 101ff. for a more detailed discussion of this criticism.
33 For a discussion of this fascinating topic see Thomas Nagel, 'Brain bisection and the unity of consciousness', 1971, in John Perry ed. *Personal Identity* (Berkeley: University of California Press, 1975), p. 231.
34 For a discussion of the possibility of personal identity surviving physical death see *Philosophy of Mind* (forthcoming) by Daniel Cardinal.

■ Chapter 10

35 Spinoza (1677), *The Ethics*, ed. and trans. R. H. M. Elwes, 2 vols (1883–84).
36 Corinthians 15: 37.
37 For example, *Phaedo* 69e–80d.
38 G. Ryle, *The Concept of Mind* (London: Hutchinson, 1949).
39 The movement was founded by Edmund Husserl (1859–1938). See, e.g., E. Husserl, *Cartesian Meditations*, trans. Dorion Cairns (The Hague, 1960); Ideas *General Introduction to Pure Phenomenology*, trans. W. R. Boyce (London: Gibson, 1931).

Selected bibliography

Cottingham, John, *Descartes*, Blackwell, 1986

Cottingham, John, *The Rationalists*, Oxford University Press, 1988

Descartes, René, *Discourse on Method and the Meditations*, tr. F. E. Sutcliffe, Penguin Classics, 1968

Dicker, G., *Descartes: An Analytical and Historical Introduction*, Oxford University Press, 1993

Perry, J. ed., *Personal Identity*, University of California Press, 1975.

Ryle, Gilbert, *The Concept of Mind*, Hutchinson, 1949

Williams, B. W., *Descartes: The Project of Pure Enquiry*, Pelican Books, 1978

Wilson, Margaret Dauler, *Descartes*, Routledge & Kegan Paul, 1978 (reprinted 1991, Routledge)

Index